Dear Sojourner

Dear Sojourner

A MEMOIR OF LESSONS ON OVERCOMING, ACHIEVING, AND THRIVING IN AND OUTSIDE COLLEGE

Ruth Olujobi

For more resources and updates, visit www.dearsojourner.com

ISBN (Paperback): 978-978-695-566-7
ISBN (eBook): 978-978-695-567-4
ISBN (Hardcover): 978-978-696-476-8

Contents

Dedication..vii

Foreword..viii

Introduction...xii

1: Arrival.. 1

2: The gift of friendship.. 9

3: Building community..22

4: Keeping your eyes on the dream.................................31

5: Excelling in your academics..40

6: Maximizing opportunities...49

7: Leadership and its weight..64

8: Taking care of yourself..78

9: Building new habits and staying accountable 92

10: Handling homesickness..99

CONTENTS

11: Dealing with rejection, loss, and failure....................104

12: Relationships and love life..114

13: Embracing your identity and loving yourself...........126

14: Navigating the Fear of Missing Out (FOMO)...........133

15: Managing your finances...145

16: Shining your light and leaving a legacy....................155

17: Preparing for life after college..................................162

18: My faith, my anchor..168

19: Staying grateful..175

20: The process of applying to U.S. colleges..................179

A note from the author..189

Acknowledgments..191

DEDICATION

To my parents and siblings:
For their unwavering support during my college journey.

To every dreamer:
I pray you never lose your passion.

FOREWORD

I wonder if a little back-story is within my job description for writing the foreword of this book. However, I trust that I will finally land on a point which resonates with you, dear reader, and which will bring you to the point where you realize that this book you are about to read is a masterpiece on the subject of excellence in a flawed world with equally flawed humans.

When Ruth reached out to me, asking if I would write the foreword for this extraordinary book, my first reaction was a slight panic. To be honest, it wasn't just a gentle, fleeting moment of nervousness. It was a full-on internal alarm bell ringing, "Why me?" Scratch that, it was "WHY ME?" in bold, blinking, capital letters. I wondered why she thought I was the right person to set the tone for a book centered around excellence, boldness, resilience, and the art (or science?) of navigating life's unpredictable twists and turns as a young adult in college.

Despite her beautifully crafted explanation of why she chose me—words full of kindness, I must say—I still wrestled with what I would call *dents on my record of success.* After all, writing the foreword for a book about achieving greatness and making excellent choices sounded like the kind of task meant for someone with an immaculate success story; someone who has scaled every mountain, conquered every fear, and smashed every goal with flair and finesse. And while I have had my share of victories (a very huge share, to be honest), my journey, like most human journeys, is not a short, straight line from ambition to achievement. It is filled with bumps, detours, doubts, and more than a few moments of wondering whether I was cut out for the race at all.

But after a lot of thinking, I realized something. Ruth chose me precisely because of *that*. She knows that I do not have a flawless record. She knows that my life, like yours and everyone else's, is a messy tie of wins and losses, laughter and tears, progress and occasional painful setbacks. She knows that I have not always gotten everything right, and that I don't always have it all figured out. But if there is one thing I have learned to do, one thing that I can share with you, dear reader, it is this: I show up.

Again and again.

Through the good days and the bad ones, through seasons of incredible clarity and blurred, foggy days, I show up. Not because I always feel ready. Not because the path is always clear. But because showing up is half the battle, maybe even more. And this is a truth that undergirds everything you are about to read.

I sometimes wonder where we humans picked up the exhausting idea that life must be lived perfectly if it'll be worthwhile. That is very strange for people who live in a world designed with seasons, eclipses, life and death, the grey color, and whatnot. The sun would, on rare occasions, have to be covered by the moon, and sometimes would not rise when we expect it to.

If you think about it more deeply, things are more beautiful and exciting because of these imperfections. The pinkness or other coloration of leaves in autumn is really because the leaves are dying and will soon fall off. How are we able to admire autumn leaves so much and expect our lives to go as planned all the time? This is the paradox of the human reality. If we can appreciate the fleeting beauty of dying leaves, the bruised look of a stormy sky, the unevenness of mountain peaks, why do we expect our lives to unfold with flawless precision? The messy parts are not deviations from the story. They are the story. It is part of the beauty of life that we are not always at 100% all the time. However, what matters is that we show up.

I have mentioned the phrase *show up* thrice within 674 words, and I prescribe it as the phrase that should keep resounding in your mind as you go through the words of this book. Why do I emphasize this? Because you stand at the doorway of adulthood, especially in these crucial college years, where you will be tempted, again and again, to believe that you must have it all figured out. You will be tempted to believe that excellence means never failing, never doubting, never feeling lost or exhausted. And you will be tempted to measure yourself against impossible standards.

Don't. Instead, remember this: what matters most is that you *show up.*

Showing up, even when you do not feel like it, even when you are uncertain, even when things seem to be falling apart, is one of the most powerful commitments you can make to yourself.

College life is a daily exercise in making choices. From the moment you wake up and are faced with deciding whether to hit snooze again or drag yourself to that early lecture to the late-night dilemmas of whether to binge-watch one more episode or finish that assignment, your life is a story shaped by countless little (but not insignificant) decisions. To study or to procrastinate. To attend a party or to prioritize rest. To nurture a friendship or to let a toxic one go. To stay true to your values or to bend to fit in. These decisions may seem small in the moment, but collectively, they carve out the path of your future.

There will be days when you feel on top of the world, unstoppable. Cherish those days; dance in the sunlight of those moments. But there will also be days when you feel drained, disillusioned, and exhausted. Days when you wonder if you are smart enough, talented enough, or brave enough. And on those days, it will be more important than ever to show up *anyway.*

Your feelings are invaluable. They are excellent messengers, giving you an idea of what is happening inside. But feelings are not designed to be your decision-makers. They are like the warning lights on a dashboard, not the steering wheel. Wisdom, not feelings, must take the lead. Perhaps you have never thought of your life in this way before, but adulthood is, at its core, an unending series of choices. Each decision carries consequences, some immediate, some delayed, some subtle, others life-altering.

In high/secondary school, many of your major life decisions were made for you, but now you are stepping into a season where your choices truly belong to you, and where their outcomes will have real-life consequences. That indeed can be terrifying, but it is also liberating. You are not powerless. You have agency. You can course-correct and evolve. This is why having a book like this is such a gift.

Ruth has, with generous thoughtfulness, taken the time to craft a guide for you; a guide which does not pretend that life is simple, or that excellence is only for the flawless. She has written honestly and practically about the areas of life that matter most in these years: academics, friendships, health, gratitude, discipline, courage, and a host of other important topics. She does not ask you to replicate her life but rather to live yours boldly, with open eyes and an open heart. She invites you to see mistakes not as failures, but as teachers. She invites you to understand that excellence is not an accident; it is a daily decision. A choice to rise and learn.

As she has rightly pointed out, you must put in the work too. Yes, Cs do have degrees too, but how would you sit with yourself knowing that you *could* have been more but just did not try?

So, as you turn these pages, dear reader, I hope you find not just good advice but a companion for the journey. May you be inspired and challenged. And above all, may you be reminded that no matter how imperfect your story may feel at times, no matter your background, what matters is that you keep showing up. Because showing up imperfectly, vulnerably, yet bravely, is where the real magic begins.

I also wonder if it is within my job description to propose a new dictionary meaning for the word *excellence as showing up despite the odds.*

Ikanna Okim
April 2025.

INTRODUCTION

During one of my work shifts in the first semester of my final year at Bowdoin, I received a familiar remark from a first-year student. She said, "Wow, Ruth! You've done so much, and I bet you have a lot to share. You should write a book!"

She and her friends had come that evening to say hi during my shift, and after a while, they began to ask me some reflective questions about my time at Bowdoin. As I responded, they asked more questions, many of which I had gotten before. I began to realize how similar many of the questions I received about my time in college were, and how many people would benefit from the lessons I have learned throughout my college journey.

A few days later, I bumped into another first-year student while walking into our Science Library, and as we chatted, we got talking about some of the things I had learned during my time at Bowdoin. She asked about the opportunities I utilized, how I was chasing my dreams, and more. Just before I said goodbye and headed in to find a space to study, she said, "You should write a book!"

I froze.

It felt like another nudge from God to do what He had been telling me to do since my second year at Bowdoin, and it was becoming increasingly clear that this was an important project to mark the end of my time at Bowdoin.

Even with all these confirmations, so to speak, at a point in writing this book, I sent two of my brothers a message saying I was worried I didn't have enough to say to make up a whole book. That worry persists even as I type this Introduction. However, I know this feeling is not unique to me. It's normal for us to feel this kind of worry when we choose to undertake projects that are bigger than anything we've ever done before. But this worry shouldn't hold us back.

Instead, we should use it as a propeller to achieve those things we dream about. Our stories are worth sharing, and we all have so much to give to the world. I'm hoping this book helps you see that your story is worth sharing, too.

The big why.

I wrote this book to share with you some of the lessons I have learned over the past four years of my life as an undergraduate in the U.S. I know I must share the gems I have found along the way and pay it forward to all the people coming behind me. As much as I would love to share my story one-on-one with everyone who has questions, I know that this is not possible, so I wrote this book to serve as a guide as you navigate your journey.

In the following pages, you will hear of how I navigated moving to the U.S. alone from Lagos, Nigeria, to start my college journey, how I built my community, and how I continued chasing my dreams after changing my environment. You'll see the many opportunities I seized and what I learned from them, how I navigated rejections, loss, taking care of myself, growing my finances, and more.

These insights will be valuable to you, and I know I would be doing the world a huge disservice if I did not share the many lessons I have learned in the last few years.

If you're a high school or college student reading this, I don't want you to long to become me—I want you to strive instead to be the best version of yourself. I know you have so much potential, so much you can be and do, so much that the world is yet to see, and I want to help you share that with the rest of the world. I know you're capable of more than you realize, so I'm here to remind you that the world is your oyster. You carry so much light, and you're meant to shine brightly. But it's okay if you don't feel like the best version of yourself now. Honestly, I don't either. We're just trying our best, day by day. I hope you can do that too—try to put in a little effort even when you feel like you're not at your best.

Navigating this book.

Some common words you will hear me mention throughout this book include:

College: This generally refers to an institution focused on undergraduate education, and it is often used interchangeably with university in the U.S.

Freshman year: my first year at Bowdoin.

Sophomore year: my second year.

Junior year: my third year.

Senior year: my final year at Bowdoin.

You will also hear me use the word *high school,* which is referred to as *secondary school* in other parts of the world. These are just a few of the words I will use that might be unfamiliar, depending on where you're reading this book from.

I encourage you to look up words or phrases you're not familiar with, if you can, so that you can get the very best from the book. I also understand that we all come from different social, economic, and religious backgrounds, so I encourage you to read this book with curiosity, openness, and a willingness to learn.

Read the book however you see fit—sequentially or bouncing around different chapters. And hey, please make use of the journaling space provided at the end of each chapter. It's to help you capture lightbulb moments or make important to-do notes you'd otherwise forget. And with that, let us begin.

CHAPTER 1

Arrival

"There are far better things ahead than any we leave behind."

— C.S. Lewis

At the airport.

I arrived in the U.S. for the very first time on August 6, 2021. I was a seventeen-year-old girl from Lagos, Nigeria, who was ready to immerse herself in the opportunities of this new world.

I remember the moment my plane landed at the huge Atlanta airport—my first stop. I stepped out with my black and blue EducationUSA school bag and my black carry-on luggage, the one my mum had purchased for me a few weeks earlier.

As I walked off the jet bridge, I couldn't believe the crowd of people I saw walking briskly between airport gates and through the enormous airport hallway. I had only an hour and a half layover (which was not a lot), so I had to make sure I was asking the right questions to go through immigration and get to my connecting flight on time.

I looked around the airport for signs on how to go from one point to another. And after about an hour and a half of going through customs, finding my checked-in luggage, and getting to my connecting flight, I was ready to jet off to Boston, where I would meet my host family. I would be staying with them until it was time to head to Bowdoin, the institution that would be making a neuroscientist out of me.

For years, I had dreamed, hoped, and prayed to study abroad, and here I was, about to start living that dream.

Back home.

I grew up in Ikorodu, a suburb in Lagos, Nigeria, with a population of about one million people, many struggling to make ends meet. During those years, I would walk to school, attending classes in the mornings and afternoons before returning home. In the evenings, I helped my mum in her little kiosk close to our home, where she sold second-hand school bags and shoes, before she transitioned to selling groceries and small household necessities.

My family was low-income, so I grew up seeing my parents work hard to fend for me and my five siblings, but there was much I didn't fully understand till I became older. Seeing how hard my parents worked and the state of things in my community made me long for more, but six-year-old me could only imagine so much without any exposure. This changed when I left home a year later.

A mind shift.

At seven, I went to live with another family, the Nwozors, because I and their only daughter at the time, who was two years younger than I, were as close as sisters.

Before I went to live with the Nwozors, I would visit their large house frequently, playing on the gorgeous ceramic floors, intrigued by the exquisite smells of the rooms. Sometimes, I would even sleep over, occasionally refusing to go home. This was why, when they moved to a different neighborhood and I wanted to follow them, my parents did not oppose it. Two of my older brothers had lived with them briefly while they attended secondary school, so my parents knew I would be alright. They also knew I'd get a good education.

I spent five of my formative years with this family and eventually returned home, having gotten a perspective on the world that I would otherwise not have.

It was while I was living with the Nwozors that I first expressed my desire to have my college education abroad. I can't remember my age then, maybe between nine or ten, but I remember one particular night in church when my friend asked me what university I wanted to attend (in Nigeria, that is) and I replied that I wanted to study abroad instead. She looked at me as if I were simply speaking about a fantasy, which was understandable, given that she also came from a low-income background. Yet, her disbelief didn't bother me. I knew what I wanted. It would be almost eight years before that dream of mine would come true.

Those five years away from home were critical in helping me dream beyond the shores of Ikorodu and shaping my mindset around who I wanted to be when I grew up.

Nurturing my dreams.

I have always wanted to be a doctor for as long as I can remember. Growing up, you would often find me sitting on the cemented floor of my parents' home, playing pretend, with the strap of my water bottle around my neck serving as the stethoscope. But it was during those years living away from home that I began to actively say I wanted to work with pregnant women, mothers, and children. My interest in Obstetrics and Gynecology had begun.

And during those years with the Nwozors, I learned to play the violin, getting my first violin at the age of ten. I joined my church's orchestra only a few weeks later and played at national church retreats with the children's church orchestra.

I flew in an airplane for the first time, too, during those years. In awe, I would look out the window at the clouds beneath us. I spent that Christmas, and a few others after, in a wealthy neighborhood in Abuja, Nigeria, with the extended family of the Nwozors. Then I'd eagerly narrate the experience to my parents each time I visited home.

This was why, when I returned home in Ikorodu at twelve to start my senior secondary school (the last three years of high school), I continued to tell my family I hoped to study outside the country. Even though I was back in this community, my perspective on the world had expanded in ways that could not be reversed.

Sadly, I had to pause playing the violin for about two years because we couldn't afford one when I returned home. But during that time, I joined the choir and gave it my all until I was gifted a violin by my eldest brother, Emmanuel, and I could rejoin the orchestra. All the while, I joined different clubs in high school, consistently growing my leadership and public speaking skills.

I remember watching Gifted Hands, a movie based on the life of Dr. Ben Carson, and telling my immediate elder brother that I, too, wanted to go to Johns Hopkins University. Things like these helped me keep dreaming, keep pushing, even on days when things were particularly hard and discouraging.

I will never forget that day I wasn't allowed into my school because my school fees hadn't been fully paid, and I went home crying. As I lay on my parents' bed, calling my eldest sister, little did I know what the future held for me.

Huge things can begin in small places.

I gave this brief context of my background to show that as someone who did not grow up with much, someone who did not have any precedent in her family for studying in the United States, or anywhere outside Nigeria at that, my journey to the U.S. was a big deal for me. It was a big deal for my family, my teachers, my community, and everyone who knew where I was coming from. My arrival in the U.S. was no ordinary arrival—it was the arrival of a dreamer-girl who had come a long way.

Standing in Boston Logan Airport after my connecting flight landed, I could not believe I had finally made it to the U.S., a country that not long ago had seemed so far away, in terms of both distance and dreams. As I waited in the baggage claim area for my two large red and black items of luggage to be sent down from my flight, I reflected on the ups and downs in my college application journey and the series of events that had led me to where I was.

I had spent the past two years tirelessly applying to colleges, and even more years working hard. It finally paid off. Oh, what indescribable joy! I was about to begin a journey that would define the rest of my life. I had arrived.

A fresh start.

There's a starting point to the college experience. We all have to arrive even to begin, and whether you're like me and you flew across the world to attend school, or you are like my siblings, schooling in your home country, the feeling of a fresh start is mutual. At that moment of arrival, you're stepping into a new door, opening yourself up to the possibilities that lie ahead of you. I fully understand how exciting but scary it can be, how you might feel or may have felt many emotions, and how many questions might be running through your mind.

The first few days of arrival are crucial in forming your college experience. This is not to say the other days don't carry heavy weight as well. I believe that the way you are welcomed into your school's community, the people who stand by your side, hold your hands, show you around, and are there for you as you figure things out, can significantly influence your experience at the school.

The afternoon I arrived in Boston, my Nigerian host family, the Obis, picked me up from the airport. My elder sister, Grace, who had attended the same graduate school as Mrs. Obi while they were both still in Nigeria, had connected me with them since I was traveling alone with no family or friends in the U.S. My sister and Mrs. Obi had maintained their relationship over the years despite their physical separation, so when I got admitted to Bowdoin and prepared to travel to the U.S., my sister reached out asking if they would be willing to look after me.

The Obis were more than happy to welcome me to the U.S., even though Bowdoin was a few states away. So for the next two weeks after I arrived in the U.S., I stayed in their home.

I cannot begin to explain how much those two weeks impacted my transition to the U.S. Being in a Nigerian home meant I got to eat home-cooked Poundo Yam and Egusi Soup, and was with a family that could relate to home and familiarly speak to my parents. I would also go on to get connected to a broader Nigerian community. Did I mention they also attended the same church I attended in Nigeria? Oh yes! So the next Sunday, I went to church with them, singing Nigerian praise songs, listening to a sermon by a pastor that could have as well been my pastor in Lagos, and receiving a warm welcome from this Nigerian community that did not just feel like home, but would soon become home.

Getting to campus.

Two Saturdays after I arrived in the U.S., my host family drove several states to drop me off at Bowdoin. Then, the afternoon I arrived on campus, one of my first-year roommates, Yanevith, had also just arrived. Standing right beside my three (or four, depending on whether you're using the American or British system) story-building dorm, she spotted me as I approached, walked up to me and my host family, introduced herself, and gave me a big hug.

She was the first person I met, and she had come to campus early for the international students' orientation. She joined us to move my things into our room and took pictures of my host family and me. Yanevith would go on to become one of my dearest friends at Bowdoin. In a moment, I'll tell you a whole lot more about building friendships and finding a community.

Facing the days ahead.

Now that you have arrived, celebrate, because there is so much ahead of you.

I had come a long way to get to Bowdoin, but that was not the end. It was just the beginning. As John Dewey said, "Arriving at one goal is the starting point to another." I still had a whole college journey ahead of me, and I had a myriad of things to navigate.

Who was I going to be friends with? Would I like the food? What classes would I take? Would I be able to find a Christian community that felt like home? How would I cope during winter? These are a few of the questions that came up in the first few days and weeks of my arrival at Bowdoin.

Adjusting to a university, whether at home or abroad, can feel different for everybody. Plus, it takes time. This period of arrival is crucial for setting the tone for the rest of your time in college. Pay special attention to it.

I know that the journey can feel like different things for different people. Maybe you are excited, worried, or overwhelmed. I understand. This is a fresh opportunity for you to build the life of your dreams. There is so much ahead of you. So much to learn, to do, to be. You're capable of more than you think, and your arrival at the start of this new chapter is a reminder of that. But you cannot go through this journey alone. I certainly couldn't.

Once I arrived, I started meeting new people and making friends. My friendships have been one of my core pillars at Bowdoin, and I have learned a lot about the roles of lifelong friendships in our lives. That's why we'll be talking about it in the next chapter.

Please make your notes here:

CHAPTER 2

The gift of friendship

"The greatest gift of life is friendship, and I have received it."

— Hubert H.

When I arrived on campus in August 2021, the first person I met was Yanevith, one of my first-year roommates and a fellow international student.

That first semester, Yanevith and I took two classes together—Brains in Motion with Professor Diaz-Rios (who became our Major Advisor) and Microhistories with Professor Cikota. We've both gone on to become close friends, sharing our experiences as women in STEM from underrepresented backgrounds, amongst other things. Our relationship was one of the first ones to show me how similar people's experiences can be despite coming from different backgrounds.

In the weeks that followed, I found and joined the Christian fellowship on campus, the African students' club, the choir, and a few more communities based on my interests. Since Bowdoin is very community-oriented, I found that there were many structures in place for first-year students to build community, but I still had to be intentional about those I was spending time with.

Friendships are important for how we show up to the world. We are social beings, so we have been made to interact with one another and belong to communities. We cannot exist alone and can only do so much without being in a community, whether that's a small or large group.
At that time, I did not know how the communities I was spending my

early days at Bowdoin with would shape the rest of my time in college. But looking back, I can see that they influenced the choice of friends I made, the way I showed up on campus, what I complained about and what I took as the norm, the places I went, and even how I saw my place on campus. I hope that if you are yet to start college and are preparing to, you'll put a lot of thought into these early days. They really can influence a lot.

I'll be sharing some lessons I've learned about fostering meaningful relationships in college and tips that can help you as you continue your journey.

Tips for fostering meaningful relationships in college:

1. Consider your values:

Over the last four years of my time at Bowdoin, I have realized that all my close friends are people with whom I share several core values. Some of my core values include my Christian faith, honesty, trust, and intentionality. Now, I said close friends, which means I have some not-so-close friends that I don't share as many values with.

That being said, I don't have any friends I don't share a significant amount of values with because I honestly don't see how a friendship could work that way. It is these shared values that will help keep the friendship going and help you continue even in rocky times. It is also what gives that friendship the ability to make you a better person.

2. Choose quality over quantity:

I've heard this phrase in the context of different things in the past few years, and one of the most frequent places has been in friendships. At the start of the first semester of my final year at Bowdoin, I had a call with a dear friend and Bowdoin alum, Onyedika. We were catching up before the semester would get too busy, and I remember how he spoke to me about being intentional about my friendships.

"Invest in the friendships you want to take with you after Bowdoin," he said, reminding me that there were only a number of people I could stay close friends with after graduation.

As someone who makes several connections, it can sometimes be challenging to know what relationships I should be channeling my energy towards. However, I had to learn that it wasn't all friendships that could be close. There were levels to the whole thing.

The reality is that we simply do not have the capacity to be close friends with everyone, even if we tried. We would end up with no close friends at all, in addition to being exhausted from trying. I've learned that it's better to nurture your relationships and make them stronger and deeper, even if they're small, than try to make a multitude of friends that you inevitably will not be able to keep up with. I know you might think it's better to have a lot of friends so you can have several people to hang out with, but trust me, it's too emotionally taxing to do so.

3. Make an effort:

"The only way to have a friend is to be one," said Ralph Waldo Emerson.

At the start of my senior year, three of my close friends and I decided we would get dinner together every other Thursday throughout that year. The name of this group was CARD—Cath, Alex, Ruth, and Daniel. We had formed this group at the end of our first year when we organized a card-writing event for the graduating seniors in our Christian fellowship.

Over the years on campus, we built our relationship, being support systems for each other, sharing our joys and pain, and helping each other grow. It had not been an easy ride, as no friendship is, but we had grown closer with every year. So when senior year came, we decided we were going to take things up a notch with our intentionality.

Along with grabbing consistent dinners, we chose to make a special kind of memory to hold onto long after we graduated. We set out to record bi-weekly podcast episodes. We called these sessions CARD Chronicles, and they were moments for us to catch up with each other and reflect on topics like our Christian faith, academics, relationships, growth, and challenges over the years.

The aim was to listen to these episodes a few years down the line, maybe in graduate school, while working, or even with our spouses and children. We wanted to capture some moments from now, moments we knew we would certainly cherish in the years to come. This level of intentionality deepened our relationship even more during our senior year.

Over the years, I have learned that friendships require a lot of intentionality. It's key for any relationship to thrive, and this can look different for everyone, especially depending on where you are in life. There will be people you're friends with just because you see them often. But lasting friendships usually go deeper than that. You would usually need to put in the work.

Now, I know that can sound daunting or overwhelming, but honestly, I don't think it's that bad. When you think about it, what meaningful thing doesn't require intentional work? And while we might not constantly feel like we can put in the necessary effort, those times should be the exception, not the norm.

4. Remember, vulnerability deepens relationships:

On one of the nights in February 2025, when I was deep in the job application grind, I responded to one of Onyedika's texts at almost two a.m. He saw it and responded a few minutes later.

Our conversation over text led to him asking why I was awake so late, and contrary to his thought that I was pulling an all-nighter for schoolwork, I was reading a book and crafting job-related emails. As he checked in on how I was doing, I mentioned that there had been many ups and downs during that season of my life and that night, I was feeling particularly stressed, which was why I couldn't sleep.

He asked if he could call, and I told him that if he did, he would just hear me cry. His response was affirming, and about a minute later, he called, listening to me de-stress and assuring me that things were going to turn out okay. After our call, I sat on my couch in gratitude, thankful I had friends I could talk to at such moments of distress. This experience was one of the many vulnerable experiences I had with friends throughout my time at Bowdoin.

You can't have deep friendships where vulnerability is missing. You should be free enough to tell your close friends matters that are close to your heart and listen to them talk about matters close to their own hearts—matters that none of you would disclose to any random person. That's vulnerability. And unless you can be that honest with the people you call friends, they're not your friends.

While I can choose to only rave about friendships, it's important to mention that they can break apart, and this is one of the reasons people might be worried about being vulnerable. The truth is: no friendship is guaranteed to last forever. So, simply because there is a possibility of the friendship falling apart is too little a reason not to invest in it. If we refused to invest in our friendships, we would end up with none.

Friends vs Acquaintances.

One cold February night, I had dinner with a sophomore at Bowdoin, and I asked her how her friendships have been. I was curious to know how she chose the current friend group she was a part of, and this topic came up: not everyone who relates well with you is your friend.

As we chatted, she said, "People might just say hi to you because they have a good perception of you, not because they're your friends."

She was spot on! I think one of the reasons we get disappointed in friendships is that we aren't aware or honest about people's places in our lives. If you're expecting lots of high energy and engagement from someone who is just an acquaintance, when you don't get that energy, you get disappointed.

The truth is that not everyone who smiles with you is your friend. People can be nice to you just because they're nice people, not because they see themselves as your friends. I had different people I knew and always said hi to on my way to class, in the dining, on the quad, and other places on campus, but they were not really my friends. They were just acquaintances.

Now, who is an acquaintance? The Merriam-Webster dictionary defines an acquaintance as a person whom one knows but who is not a particularly close friend. I think that not making this distinction between friends and acquaintances is something that can hurt us and leave us feeling disappointed in a relationship. We might not realize we are expecting more from it than it really is, and might be putting in more effort than the relationship requires.

Friendship due to proximity.

There is such a thing as *friends due to proximity,* and this is something I didn't realize until my junior year. These are the friendships you have because you bump into those people a lot, not because you would go out of your way to be friends with them, nor would you stay in touch if you were no longer in the same location.

You might bump into them on your way to class, the dining hall, the store, etc., but those are the only times you speak with them. Yes, you might say, "Let's catch up soon" or "Let's grab a meal sometime," ever so often, but you never do, because you are not actually that close with them. Those phrases serve more as greetings than actual offers. You just say it to say it, but you don't need to mean it.

It's important to recognize when a friendship is just due to proximity, because it can predict the duration of that relationship, which might influence your interactions with the person involved. If there are friendships of this sort coming to your mind, but you want to strengthen them, consider finding ways to deepen the relationship. Beyond just exchanging pleasantries whenever you meet, be intentional about finding time to connect. This can transform that relationship and give you something more than a superficial friendship.

Long-distance friendships.

Since coming to the U.S. in 2021, I have formed more long-distance friendships than I had anticipated. One special set of long-distance friendships I gained happened in the summer of 2023 and has continued to flourish since then.

I traveled home to intern at the Lagos University Teaching Hospital (LUTH) in Lagos, Nigeria, and during that period, I connected with students at the medical school the hospital was affiliated with—the College of Medicine, University of Lagos (CMUL).

A few days before the start of my internship, I received a message on Instagram from Daniel Afolabi, a pharmacy student at CMUL, who had been following me on the platform before then. His message was intriguing, and since I was going to be on campus for a few weeks, we set out time to meet. The day came, and I finally met Daniel, but our conversation that day felt like we had known each other for longer.

We spoke about how he started following me on Instagram, courtesy of one of our mutual friends, Victor Onuh, why I was at home for the summer, his writing interests, my podcast, and much more. By the end of our meeting, I knew I was gaining a lifelong friendship.

A few days earlier, I had bumped into Ife, a medical student at CMUL whom I had connected with online in 2020 but had never met in person until then. I was going to complete my internship registration, and as I walked into CMUL's main gate with my dad, there she was, about to walk out.

Although we had not physically met until that moment, we instantaneously recognized each other, and the next thing you know, we were screaming each other's names and hugging each other. After about three years of knowing her, I was finally meeting her in person. A few weeks later, we went out to catch up with how we were both doing and got to spend time with each other. It strengthened our relationship in a way we had not expected.

Several weeks later, I visited CMUL for the last time before returning to the U.S. My internship that summer had ended, so I came to say bye to Deola, a family friend and medical student at CMUL. As she finished her class and came out to meet me, a friend of hers and fellow medical student who had begun following me on Instagram a few weeks earlier, courtesy of Daniel, came along and introduced himself.

We immediately struck up a conversation and exchanged contacts before I left, so we could speak more and keep in touch. This was how I met my now good friend, Timilehin. But Timilehin was not the only person I met through Daniel that summer. Twice during my internship, I spoke with Gabriel, another of Daniel's friends, whom I stayed connected with even after I returned to the States.

My friendships with students at CMUL have grown since then, with me meeting Bukola, an incredible friend, pharmacy student (and editor, if I may add), and Esther, a fellow amazing pharmacy student.
I'm sharing to show you that we don't have to lose our friendships when we move far away, and even when we are in a place for only a brief period, like I was at LUTH, we can still nurture our friendships.

On my twenty-first birthday, many of my friends in CMUL, and Tunmise, a wonderful friend of mine at the University of Lagos's main campus, came together to create a wholesome birthday video. This touched me deeply because they reminded me how much my community and friendships with them have flourished despite the distance.

Long-distance friendships hold so much beauty, and it would be such a loss to let them go because of distance. Despite the hurdle that distance might present, these friendships can be deeply enriching and wax stronger as the years go by.

Confronting hard things in friendship.

I remember one of the bitterly cold nights in the spring semester of my senior year when one of my friends came to my Duty Night. Duty Nights are Residential Life shifts where a Residential Life student staff member creates a welcoming and often fun space in the common room of first-year dorms for students to hang out between nine p.m. to two a.m. on Fridays and Saturdays.

As we came in and sat down, she propped her legs on the couch while she rested her head. I knew that was not a good idea because her shoes were most likely dirty with all the slush and salt from the dissolving snow, so I encouraged her to put her legs down. She didn’t, even after I mentioned it again, so I didn’t mention it anymore. A few minutes later, she got up from the chair to use the bathroom, and when she returned, I gestured to the stains on the chair from her boots. She had to spend a few minutes scrubbing the couch because we both knew she couldn’t leave it that way.

I think I am that annoying friend who reprimands her friends. I promise you: I always do it with the best intentions. My closest friends at Bowdoin have teased me that I act like a mum, but they're not just the ones who say so. I’ve been hearing it as far back as when I was in the children's choir back in Lagos. Some of my friends would go as far (maybe too far) as calling me a grandma in tribute to my guiding and motherly nature, if you will.

While I recognize that this can be annoying, I’ve also heard, over the years, how thankful my friends are that I tell them things they might not necessarily want to hear. To me, this is one of the main things friendship is about—keeping each other accountable. I think it's much easier to tell each other how great the other person is; it's easier to say how much you appreciate their presence in your life; and easier to say how much you love them. But when it comes to giving feedback or saying uncomfortable truths, that can be challenging.

I think this is particularly so for our closest friendships and relationships because we might feel we have a lot to lose if the feedback is not accepted well. It's normal to worry about our friendships being negatively impacted when we mention these hard things, but I believe that true friendships involve sharpening each other, which comes from having tough but necessary conversations.

We can't build deep friendships by avoiding these uncomfortable conversations. You'll just have a superficial friendship that you probably inwardly resent. If you always shy away from telling your friends the things they need to hear, then the truth is that you are not true friends; you simply have a friendship of convenience.

There's a flip side, too. If you don't have friends who are willing to tell you areas you need to grow, then that's a red flag. How can you become a better version of yourself when your friends won't tell you the ways you need to improve? I know you might be worried about losing your friend because of these hard conversations, but the friendships that can work through these difficult but important conversations are the ones that often last the longest.

Friendships can change.

I cannot speak about friendships without acknowledging that they can change and even end. This is something that can be hard to grapple with, but it's the reality of life. There's a quote by Tyrese Gibson I have heard a few times, and it goes: "People are in your life for a reason, others are there for a season, and it's important to realize when those seasons are over."

There are several people I was friends with in high school whom I barely speak to now. We might send a check-in text once every few months, we might leave a comment on each other's posts, we might celebrate with each other online when something major happens in our lives (and we post about it), but our relationship is nowhere as close as it used to be. Some of these friendships changed because we no longer saw each other as often, we were no longer a part of the communities that brought us together, our values changed, or life simply went on, and we developed other relationships.

As we grow, our friendships evolve and change. Some grow stronger and become an integral part of our lives, but others can change from friendship to acquaintances.

Some days, when I revisit the memories from my childhood and teenage friendships—the friendships that made my formative years memorable—I become nostalgic and wish I could have all of those friendships back. But I know that it is not possible to maintain all my friendships throughout my life. People come and go, and that's okay. Instead of trying to hold on to all my old friendships, I ask myself who I would love to reconnect with and how I can be a good friend in the moment. I hope you'll also reflect on that question.

Rekindling old relationships.

"A strong social capital is not informed only by the people you meet going forward. The quality people in your past can also be very instrumental to your future." This striking statement was made by my dear friend, Oluwapelumi Ikuomenisan.

Friends come and friends go, yes. But sometimes some friends might feel gone, but aren't. They're just a text away. This is something Pelumi reminded me of in February 2025 when we were speaking about reconnecting with old friends. We agreed that it is just as important to reflect on our old friendships and networks as it is to strive to build new ones.

I know that as we grow older and move to various places or step into different phases of our lives, we will build new connections and make new friends. This is normal, and even necessary, because we need to have relationships in the new phases of our lives. However, building these relationships doesn't have to completely replace the old ones. And what's more? We can rekindle old friendships we know are meaningful to us.

I find that whenever there is an old friend I want to reconnect with, a call, or even a thoughtful text, goes a long way. It might be that the only reason you stopped speaking with that person was that the event that brought you together had passed, or they changed their phone number, but with the digital age we're in, if you want to reconnect with someone, you can do so pretty easily.

Over the years, I have experienced the beauty of long-lasting friendships, and I can say, without a shadow of doubt, that they make life more satisfying. It's beautiful to be able to experience life with people over a span of years, to have friends that you can grow with, friends you can reflect with, and say, "Look how far we've come!" I believe that being intentional about building lasting relationships will help us live more robust lives, and I hope you become intentional about this.

Now that we have spoken about friendships, we need to speak about what it's like to have multiple people and social spaces in your life that serve you in different ways. Community is a crucial part of navigating life as a college student, and we can only go so far without it. So, how did I build my community, and how can you do it too? We'll explore that in the next chapter.

Please make your notes here:

CHAPTER 3

Building community

"One of the marvelous things about community is that it enables us to welcome and help people in a way we couldn't as individuals."

—Jean Vanier

I have found that there are many ways to build community, and quite interestingly, some of those ways play out unexpectedly.

The first place I found a community was the international students group. Being in a community with other students who had flown across the world to attend college in a small community in Maine came with a kind of unspoken understanding of the experiences of being an international student. However, I soon realized that the experiences of international students could be vastly different.

My experience as a Nigerian student was very different from my close friend from the UK. Yes, we were both on student visas; however, we were coming from different backgrounds, cultures, political climates, etc. Yet, despite these differences, we were similar. We had chosen to leave our home countries to study in the United States, and this was an experience that brought us together.

The next—and probably biggest—place I found community was in my Christian fellowship at the Joseph and Alice McKeen Study Center, fondly called JAMS. I could spend a whole day speaking about how much this community shaped my time at Bowdoin and helped me grow as a person, Christian, leader, and friend.

My first introduction to JAMS was on a Sunday afternoon after church. It was at the beginning of the fall semester of my freshman year, and I was having lunch outside Moulton with a few other students who had attended church with me. Josh, then a senior, asked the first-year students if we wanted to join JAMS' Wednesday Bible Study. I agreed. From the first Bible Study I attended, I knew I had found a solid community. And the rest, they say, is history.

You need to be in a community. You really do. And I understand you may not know your community at first, but you can't go about this life without a community to lean on. You need to find your people, whether ten, five, or three. You certainly cannot do life alone.

Support systems.

We need people who believe in us, people who will help carry our vision even when we think we cannot.

I remember the day I decided I was going to write a book during my Sophomore year at Bowdoin. The excitement was welling up in me so much that I had to record a voice note so I wouldn't forget all that was on my mind. Right after I did so, I sent it to my immediate elder brother, Stephen, so he could check in with me about it later on. Then, I told my eldest brother because I knew he would be more than happy that I was writing a book.

The summer after that school year ended, I visited home for my internship at CMUL. I was able to speak with two Lawyers I highly respect—Ikanna Okim and Gideon Edem—and I shared my hope of writing a book while in school with them. I didn't have a timeline back then and wasn't completely sure of what I wanted to write about, but I was feeling strongly led to write a book.

The day I told Ikanna about my plans to write a book, we were sitting in a restaurant, surrounded by the bustling energy of Lagos. As I shared my goals of writing a book with her, she asked what I thought of publishing the book as I was graduating, and frankly, I thought that was too far. In my mind, there was no way I would be working on the book project that long. I was wrong.

But I'm not going to blame younger me for thinking I would have published the book in my third year. The thoughts of the book came to my mind often during that summer, so I thought that by the time the school year came around, I would have worked on the book. Looking back, I realize I did not have the toolset I now have and still had a lot to experience—a lot that I can now share with you.

Apart from the people who believed in my dreams, I received support from people who knew how late I would stay at my desk working—my first-year and sophomore year roommates. I remember a night during my freshman year when I had a paper due for my first-year seminar, but I hadn't finished it yet, so I tried to pull an all-nighter. My roommates, Katharine, Sammi, and Yanevith, were very concerned and rallied beside me to support me through that rough season and the challenging times that followed.

And in my sophomore year, I would do debriefs about my days with one of my roommates, Carolina, whenever we were both in our kitchen together at night. This would often help me process my day and make me less stressed when I had lots of work to do.

It's beautiful to look back and see how much my interactions with my roommates those first two years at Bowdoin provided support, and even when I lived without roommates by junior and senior year, the relationships I had with my roommates from previous years continued.

I'm forever grateful for all the people who have helped me become who I am today, all the people who have poured into my life and helped me see beyond what I could. I'm grateful for the people who opened up platforms for me and gave me the space to shine, fully and wholly. We all need people like that.

Networking.

I have noticed that people often have different reactions to the word *networking.* Some people shiver at the thought of it and associate it with sending someone a message on LinkedIn or sending a cold email. Some people do it and are mildly comfortable with it, and some people have grown to see it as simply making connections. Whatever you currently see it as, networking, in simple terms, is a process of building and maintaining relationships.

Although these relationships are often thought of as career-centered, they go beyond a professional scope. They apply to other people in your life, such as your family members, friends, neighbors, colleagues, acquaintances, and more. Your network is all the people who shape your life in different ways, not just your career.

Growing up, I would hear the quote "Your network is your net worth" at career events, but I never really knew what that meant. *What do the people I know have to do with my net worth?* I would think. I didn't even know what my supposed net worth meant. It was foreign to me. I thought the conversation about net worth was only something for adults and people who were earning money. You know how you see those headlines about how a person has reached a $10 million net worth? That's all I associated net worth with—how much a person earned. It wasn't until I got to college that I truly understood what that statement means.

While net worth generally means a person's overall financial position and possessions, this quote was referring to something more than financial possessions. This statement was meant to show that the relationships you build can greatly influence the opportunities and resources you have access to, the spaces you enter, and your overall success. Having a robust network can lead to more open doors in terms of jobs, partnerships, mentorships, and more. These can all then lead to financial success and overall well-being.

Building your network is paramount and is an important part of your college experience. The wider your network, the more spaces and opportunities you will have access to.

I know networking can feel daunting depending on your experience or background, so I hope this chapter offers valuable insights as you navigate the process. After four years of networking as a college student, here are a few lessons I have found valuable:

1. You're not the only one networking:

I know it might not seem like it, but do you know the people you're reaching out to are also reaching out to people? Think about it for a second. We all need people, regardless of what stage we're at, and so we constantly need to reach out to people. Even those you are reaching out to are reaching out to other people as well. Regardless of how far we go in life, we will need to meet new people and form new connections. So trust me, you're not in this alone.

2. Many people are willing to help people who are showing effort:

Mmanti Umoh, one of my mentors for many years, took me on as her mentee without me directly asking to be mentored by her. I worked for an organization, Upsurge Global, that invited her to an event. I attended the event and showed that I was doing my best with what I knew. Over time, she took me under her wings and began to mentor me—something I will forever be grateful for.

As I grew, I realized that many people who have gone ahead are eager to help people who show genuine interest and look like they've been putting in the work. This has been my case in many situations, and I'm so grateful for all the people who have gone ahead of me and on whose shoulders I have sat.

3. It's only awkward if you make it awkward:

I first heard this phrase as it relates to approaching romantic relationships, but I think it applies to networking as well. When reaching out to a person, don't enter the conversation assuming it will be awkward. If you do, it will reflect in your text, voice, or email. Again, you're not the only person networking, and if done correctly, you can get a lot out of it.

Tips for Networking Successfully:

1. Prepare ahead of time:

When you attend an event where you have an organizer, speaker, or attendee you want to connect with, doing your research about them is important. Do they have any books or papers they have written that you can reference in your conversation? Did they say something interesting in a recent post they made? Did they say something at another event that spoke to you? Preparing ahead of time will allow you to show them that you have done some work and are eager to connect.

2. Find a point of connection:

When reaching out to someone for the first time, it can be helpful to establish a point of connection with them. This can be how you heard of them, if someone recommended them to you, whether you have read or watched any of their works, etc. This immediately establishes some form of connection and makes you less of a stranger to the person you are reaching out to.

3. Ask thoughtful questions and listen attentively:

When networking, asking good questions helps you show interest and makes the other person more likely to be invested in you as well. And while they speak, ensure to pay attention, so that you can make thoughtful comments and ask compelling follow-up questions. As someone who asks a lot of questions, I can tell you that people are usually impressed when you ask questions that show that you were not only listening to them, but have some interest in what they were saying. This can help you in building long-lasting connections and expanding your network.

4. Make it easy for the other person:

I have heard several times how important it is *not* to send a mere "Hi" or "Hello" text when you are connecting with a person for the first time. A mere "Hi" with nothing else accompanying it gives no context; it doesn't communicate why you're reaching out and will require the person you are connecting with to respond to you without any understanding of who you are and why you are reaching out. Instead, send a robust text introducing yourself, how you know them, and why you are hoping to connect with them. You can do this with something called an elevator pitch.

5. Crafting an elevator pitch:

> *"Hi, my name is Ruth Olujobi, and I am a senior at Bowdoin College studying Neuroscience. I am passionate about access to quality healthcare and have been involved in healthcare advocacy and communications for almost five years.*
>
> *I saw that you recently gave a talk on building equitable healthcare systems in Africa, and I was intrigued by the points you made. I would love to connect to speak more about your career path and the impact you are making."*

I wrote this elevator pitch in one go, and it was a reminder that just like any other skill, giving a good elevator pitch comes with practice. From my elevator pitch above, you might be able to tell what an elevator pitch is. It is simply a concise and compelling introduction of who you are and what you do.

Elevator pitches are usually thirty to sixty seconds long and are meant to help you make connections within a short time frame. The content of your elevator pitch will vary based on who you are speaking to, but the format is largely the same if you are networking. Ideally, it should contain your name, who you are, what you are interested in or have done, how you know this person, and an action point or request.

The more you practice, the better you get at introducing yourself, and the more confident you will feel in giving your elevator pitch. Write down your elevator pitch in the reflection page after this chapter and practice saying it out loud, either to yourself or to someone else, and refine it until you feel satisfied with it. You want to practice enough that you can say all you need to say without fumbling over your words.

Up next, we'll speak about chasing your dreams, which is the hallmark of college life.

Please make your notes here:

CHAPTER 4

Keeping your eyes on the dream

"Too many of us are not living our dreams because we are living our fears."

—Les Brown

If you knew or met me during the pandemic in 2020, you'll know that I spoke about working with the World Health Organization (WHO) a lot. I remember a career session I hosted for Upsurge Global in June 2020. I was sitting in the living room of our community nurse's home because there had not been electricity for days, and I needed to charge my phone so I could host the event.

During that session, Mmanti Umoh asked us what our career goals were and called on me to answer. I mentioned that I hoped to work with the WHO in the near future, helping to make policies that would improve the lives of people in underserved communities around the world.

My response stemmed from my passion for quality healthcare, something that had been influenced by both my personal experiences and my observations of Nigeria's healthcare system.

Growing up, I would watch how doctors related to patients anytime I was at the hospital. I would ask the doctors questions when they were attending to me, and listen intently as they suggested further tests or gave a diagnosis.

As I grew older, I began to understand the sad and serious issue of brain drain that Nigeria was facing. Every year, thousands of doctors, lawyers, and a plethora of other skilled workers and recent grads leave the country to find systems they believe value them more. This brain drain is an issue Nigeria has been experiencing for years. The exodus of experts like doctors translates to a burden on the healthcare workers left in the country. And it has been heartbreaking. Seeing how deeply I cared confirmed that working in healthcare was a big dream of mine, and I had to hold on to this dream.

Until coming to Bowdoin, I didn't know that part of the things I was passionate about was public health, but I knew I wanted to work in an organization that served underprivileged communities around the world, and the WHO was the most famous one I knew. The more I have grown in my knowledge of impactful healthcare, though, the more my preferences on where I want to work and why have shifted.

Learning about public health opened a new array of possibilities for me and showed me that there was still much about my career path I didn't yet know. I realized that our dreams can change, expand, or take a different outlook. And that's okay. Despite how my view on where I want to work and why has changed, I have remained intentional about finding ways to keep pursuing my healthcare dreams.

As I reflect on how closely I had pursued my aspirations throughout my time at Bowdoin, a few questions come to mind. They might help you as you navigate your own journey.

- ***What are your dreams, and why do they matter to you?***
- ***How long have you had these aspirations?***
- ***What would happen if you decided to go another route?***

These are questions you need to constantly ask yourself on your journey to becoming the person you want to be. And the beautiful thing with keeping your dream, your vision, in front of you, is that you'll find ways to make it happen. You'll find avenues to take baby steps and even giant steps towards it.

Let me tell you of one of the biggest things I did at Bowdoin to continue chasing my dreams of becoming a doctor.

Launching Blooming Daily.

Many people know that I started Blooming Daily in my first year at Bowdoin, but fewer know that it was not the first wellness show I would be launching. On an afternoon in August of 2020, I launched my very first health and wellness show called Teen Health TV. It was a show I would host as one of the young leaders at Teennation, the youth empowerment organization I had joined a few months prior.

Teen Health TV was a weekly show I held on Instagram Live that addressed various subjects about teen health and wellbeing. This period was the start of my second-gap year after graduating from high school, and for months, I had been thinking of ways I could continue to hone my public speaking skills and deepen my expertise in healthcare, even though I hadn't even gone to college, let alone become a doctor. I knew there had to be something I could do, a way I could contribute. So, after weeks of brainstorming, I started Teen Health TV. This was my way of tackling the issue of inadequate access to quality healthcare information.

For the next eight months, I hosted the show on Thursdays at four p.m. On those days, I would show up whether I felt prepared or not and speak about topics from exercise to healthy eating and how to build healthy habits. I even remember one afternoon when there had not been electricity for days. I tried to get a power bank to charge my phone, but I couldn't find one, so I ran to a friend's house because their side of the community had electricity at the time.

I sat in her house, and a few minutes later, there I was saying, "Hello, everyone. Welcome to this week's episode on Teen Health TV." I deeply enjoyed hosting this show and did it regardless of where I was. And even when I began to have internet issues, I pivoted to pre-recording the videos so that the show would go on.

A few weeks after I started pre-recording the videos, my phone began to have storage issues that made it hard for me to continue recording. And so after eight months of running the show, I brought it to an end. It was the end of an era, but that seed of hosting a show had been planted in me, and I did not realize this seed would sprout a year later, during my second semester at Bowdoin.

Finding my feet was all I did those first few months at Bowdoin. But once I began to feel settled, my passion for quality healthcare and speaking about health and wellness had me yearning for a platform to help me keep channeling that energy. As the end of 2021 approached, I gradually began to remember that in 2020, I had spoken about starting a podcast, and in my check-in email to Onyedika around May 2021, I signed off with your *celebrity podcaster.*

That was how I began seriously considering starting a wellness podcast, which set me off to months of brainstorming. I wrote several pages of ideas, outlining what I wanted the podcast to be, potential topics, the skills I'd need to be able to host the podcast well, what platforms I would have it on, etc.

In January 2022, I had a call with one of my elder brothers, Stephen, about wanting to start a podcast. I told him I was worried. Why? I didn't have everything figured out.

He told me something that propelled me to go ahead even though I didn't feel completely ready, and I know it'll help you too. He said, "We can never be fully ready, and if we wait till we are, we will end up not doing anything." He also told me that whether I launched the podcast or not, time would pass. Did I want to look back a year later and wish I had done it earlier? After that night, I made more preparations to launch the podcast. I connected with Promise Akpan, a phenomenal designer, who would then go on to handle Blooming Daily's brand identity.

On March 29, 2022, we officially launched Blooming Daily. I remember the excitement from siblings, my friends, and even strangers who were finding out. The vision that was once in my head had finally come to life. Blooming Daily was here and ready to thrive!

As of March 2025, Blooming Daily has published twenty-five

episodes spanning four seasons with twenty-five guests in and outside Bowdoin's community. Our episodes have been streamed from thirty-five countries, with listeners in places like Norway, Belarus, Japan, France, Mexico, Vietnam, the U.K., Brazil, Ukraine, and more! I can only imagine how much I would have missed out on if I allowed my worry of not having it all figured out hold me back, or if I didn't find a new way to keep chasing my dreams.

So I'll repeat what I said earlier. Keeping your dream in mind, answering the questions—what are your dreams and why do they matter to you?—will ensure you notice opportunities to keep chasing them.

Self-belief and self-doubt.

We doubt ourselves all the time; it's a part of human nature. And a statement that has guided me on this subject of self-doubt is the one Chimamanda Ngozi Adichie made at Harvard in 2018 during a commencement speech, where she said, "The truth is that you cannot create anything of value without both self-doubt and self-belief. Without self-doubt, you become complacent. Without self-belief, you cannot succeed. You need both."

This phrase has stuck with me because I believe that we all need self-doubt and self-belief to produce good work, and this book you're holding is no exception.

I needed to believe in myself enough to think I could pursue such a grand goal—write a whole book, and hope for it to travel around the world, bringing clarity and inspiring lives. But I also needed that self-doubt to help me not get content with putting out mediocre work. I think self-doubt allows us to strive to put in the work, which can then result in quality results. But I'm aware of the complexities of balancing self-doubt and self-belief.

Having only self-belief might hinder you from seeing the places you need improvement, and too much self-doubt could stop you from even trying at all. So, there's a need for balance. And I will admit that finding that balance can be challenging. However, I believe this balance changes at various points in our lives, and not always having that balance figured out is real and probably what we will feel most of the time! This book is a testament to the fact that when we find that balance between self-doubt and self-belief, when we chase our goals despite how humongous they might feel, we are capable of achieving so much.

The danger of becoming too comfortable.

The first few months after I arrived at Bowdoin, I had to adjust to constantly having some necessities I did not have back at home in Nigeria. Electricity was one of them. Unlike when I was home and constantly had to calculate when and how to charge my devices and how long I would be able to use them, I wasn't thinking about such things at Bowdoin. This was just one of the different things I did not have to worry about now that I was at Bowdoin.

What I realized is: when we have many of the things we once struggled to get, there is a danger of becoming too comfortable in our new environment. However, beyond getting these basic amenities, the fact that I wasn't applying to get into schools in the U.S., the fact that my big dream of coming abroad for college had finally been accomplished, seemed like a license to relax and not put as much energy into the things I was once interested in. Of course, it's important to take breaks, relax, and get refreshed, but that shouldn't mean letting go of the passions we once had.

This was something I had to be careful of.

Getting too comfortable might mean not chasing after our dreams like we used to, settling for less, not caring about the things or people that mean so much to us, and more. Whatever the case might be, it is important to do a constant self-assessment and make sure we're on track and not slipping away from things we should be channeling our energy into.

The state of being too comfortable differs from person to person, so I encourage you to find out what it means for you, so you can identify when it is happening.

Handling fear.

When I decided to write this book, one of the major things that slowed me down was fear. I was worried I did not have enough to say to make a book, that it might not work out as I had hoped, that I would not be able to finish in time, you name it. It felt like there were more hindrances to writing this book than I could surmount, but that was simply not true.

So I spoke to my support system. I told my brothers, and they did not hesitate to remind me that fear was natural when doing anything that seemed bigger than us. I texted another person I respect, Ikanna, and she immediately told me that the fear was not real. I spoke with Daniel and Bukola, two of my incredible friends who helped with editing the first draft, and they did not hesitate to let me know that the reason I was writing this book and all it was set to do was greater than any fear I might be feeling.

Growing up, I had learned that fear was simply a False Experience Appearing Real (FEAR). I spoke to more people about how I felt and continued to write. I knew the stakes for this book were high, and I did not want to take it lightly.

We all will face fears at some point or another. What determines what will result from the experience is how we respond to the fear we feel. So, like Sheryl Sandberg asked in her book *Lean In,* "What would you do if you weren't afraid?" I'm also still trying to answer this question for myself, but one thing I do know is that regardless of where I am, I need to keep chasing my dreams. I hope you will, too. And, I think you should use the next page to answer the following questions:

- ***What are your dreams, and why do they matter to you?***
- ***How long have you had these aspirations?***
- ***What would happen if you decided to go another route?***
- ***Lastly, what would you do if you weren't afraid?***

Please make your notes here:

CHAPTER 5

Excelling in your academics

"Success is the sum of small efforts, repeated day in and day out."

—Robert Collier

"Ruth, remember to prioritize your academics. It'll stay with you for a long time" is something my eldest brother was constantly reminding me throughout my time in college.

My brother would tell me several times that my grades would always stay with me, so it was important to put in my best while I could, because I would never be able to go back to correct them. This reminder was important for me to keep working hard.

The truth is: I was not obsessed with my grades. I wanted good grades, yes, but I didn't make them the entirety of my time at Bowdoin. I think this was why when I didn't get all the A's I was working and praying hard for in my first three years in college, it didn't take away from my experience at Bowdoin.

Each semester, I started on a fresh slate and set out to do my best. I tried my hardest semester after semester, combining academics with my on-campus jobs, extracurricular activities, relationships, and more. And then, one night, I saw a result that would forever stay in my mind.

It was the evening of January 3, 2025, and I was visiting Lagos, Nigeria, for my winter break. I was on the bus on my way home from a meeting when I received an email that the grades for the fall 2024 semester were out. My heart began to race because the results were out earlier than I had expected, and I had high hopes.

I texted Stephen, my immediate elder brother, telling him the results were out and saying I would like to check them with him when I got home. This was a big deal for me; it would be the first time I was checking my results with a sibling, and while at home. A few hours later, I arrived home and was ready to check my results. I asked my brother if he could make a reaction video because I wanted to capture and cherish that moment for as long as I could.

I opened my email, scanned the instructions, and logged into my portal. This was it. This was the moment I would see if I had gotten the kind of results I had never gotten before. This was a historical moment. I logged into my portal and scrolled to the section with my grades. What did I see?

All A's!

My heart was so full!

This was my first all-A's semester, and I was overjoyed! I texted my siblings and about three friends with crying emojis, telling them the personal milestone I had just achieved. This wasn't just a personal win, it was a community win.

Key parts of excelling academically:

1. Cultivating the right study habits:

Throughout my time at Bowdoin, I realized that it is impossible to succeed academically without the right study habits. Your habits determine the outcome, whether we're thinking about your academics or life in general. So if you have habits that give you the time to study well, to fully understand what you are learning, you stand a better chance of getting results you will be proud of. Good study habits include time management, taking notes, setting goals, and more. These will help you with achieving your goal academically.

2. Understanding your learning style and adapting to new ones:

We all learn differently, and it is important to understand how you learn best. Are you someone who likes to have things written or drawn out? Are you a visual learner? An audio learner? What are the ways you learn that you notice help you retain the information better? These are some of the questions you can ask when thinking about your learning style.

However, it is important to know that how you *learn best* might not be the best way to learn a particular subject. I once read in Adam Grant's *Hidden Potential* that for retaining information, most people learn better by reading than by listening. This is because with reading, we engage more with the material we are learning.

This is a reminder to keep an open mind about learning styles you might not be familiar with because they could be more effective than you realize.

3. Asking for help:

I grew up in an academic environment where asking for help was not the norm. This was further deepened by the stories my siblings told of their college days, where professors were unapproachable, and they had to always figure things out themselves or with friends. So when I got to Bowdoin, and I was encouraged to ask for help, this felt unnatural. Asking for help felt like showing weakness, and I didn't want to do that.

What I realized was that asking for help enables us to become better at that thing we need help with. The truth is: even after four years of hearing it's okay, and even important, to ask for help, I still struggle with it. Sometimes it feels like I'm making excuses when I ask for help, even when I clearly need it. I'm learning to reach out for help because that way, I can perform at my best.

4. Having a support system:

One of the first all-nighters I pulled was with two of my friends in my first semester at Bowdoin. We were in the same first-year writing seminar and had a paper to write that the three of us had procrastinated until the deadline, which was the next day. So, we sat in one of the rooms in the basement of my first-year dorm, Moore Hall, and typed away. Yanevith, yes, my roommate, was a part of that trio, alongside Sebastian. We would then go on to call ourselves the Gummy Bears because we almost always sat beside each other in class and would frequently grab meals together.

Another person who was an important source of academic support for me was Sarah. Throughout my junior year, Sarah and I studied Organic Chemistry together—often in my room, sometimes in classrooms around campus, and once in our hotel room at a conference in Burlington, Vermont. Organic Chemistry was certainly not an easy course, so I can't imagine what it would have been like to study for it alone. Now, Sarah and I have core memories from our many study sessions together.

In the chapter on community, we spoke about the importance of a support system. This same concept of having a support system is integral for doing well academically. You need people who would fill you in if you missed a class, who you can study with, who you can speak to when things don't go as planned, and who can support you when you are struggling. Having a support system can be just what you need to get you from almost reaching your academic goals to crossing the line.

5. Learning from those who have gone ahead of you:

I cannot overstress how valuable the experiences of those who have gone ahead of you can be. They know study strategies that work, how professors like students to engage, all of which can be very valuable to you. I know it can feel like an inconvenience to seek assistance from those who have gone ahead of you, but many times, people are willing to help you if you show effort. So don't be afraid to reach out.

6. Setting your goals:

"C's still get degrees" is something someone once told me when I spoke about the importance of aiming for good grades. I was immediately taken aback. She was trying to speak about the importance of not caring too much about grades because they are not the only things that matter, which is true, but something about that phrase made me uncomfortable. I understand that life happens, and this can lead to getting C's in a course, but I didn't want to accept that phrase, so I wouldn't aim lower than my current goals. C's, indeed, do get degrees, but if that is not what you want, then why settle?

Navigating time management.

Knowing how to manage your time in college is a skill that is important not just for your academics, but your entire college experience. You have a finite amount of time, so if you are engaged in one activity, it means there are other things you are not doing. This isn't a bad thing, rather, it's something to be aware of. To excel in your academics, you need to be intentional about how you are spending your time. You need to carve out time to study, catch up on classes you missed, ask questions about topics you are not clear on, and more.

It can be hard to find the time to study as much as you want while participating in extracurricular activities, spending time with your friends, managing a job if you have one, having fun, and taking care of yourself. I struggled with this myself at different points in college.

What I have found is that my time management is usually a reflection of my priorities. The things I spent the most time on at any point in time, whether I realized it or not, were the things I was prioritizing. Sometimes, my priorities were in the right order, but other times they were not, which led to me losing sleep, feeling stressed, or not getting things done in time.

Your priorities will constantly change, and it will be more evident in some seasons than others. When you are writing exams, for example, you might need to dial down on the time you are spending on your extracurricular activities. Knowing when to increase or decrease the amount of time you are giving certain activities is something you will learn as you go on.

In the first semester of my senior year, I travelled to a wedding in California, a state many miles away from Bowdoin. I travelled two days to the start of the end-of-semester exams. I did this because being at that particular wedding was important to me. I could have chosen to spend those two extra days studying for my exams, but instead I embraced the challenges of studying while in transit so I could be at the wedding with four of my friends from Bowdoin who were also travelling for the wedding.

This was something I could pull off because I had taken the right steps before we travelled. I also tried to study on the way to the wedding, even though that was almost impossible to do. When we returned to campus at midnight, leading to the first day of exams, I felt incredibly content that we had attended the wedding. I made a core memory with my friends that I will cherish for the rest of my life.

When at a crossroads on how to allocate your time or what to prioritize, ask yourself what is more important to you in that moment and in the long run. If the answers to both questions are the same, then you know what to do. If the answers are different, you will need to ask yourself what the consequences would be if you choose one over the other. If there is an obvious consequence of not doing something, like not studying for an exam the next day, or not working on an application that is due at the end of the week, then you know what needs to be done.

However, there might not always be obvious consequences of doing one thing over another. For example, you might need to decide between hanging out with a friend or going to see a show. In that case, you could go for what feels the most important to you at that moment. The key thing is to make sure that you are setting your priorities right and you are not sacrificing time you could have spent on vital activities on less important things.

Taking your learning beyond the classroom.

It wasn't until I got to the U.S. that I fully understood the importance of internships and getting experience either during breaks or even during the school year. You can't stay in the classroom forever; you have to take your learning out and utilize it. This is the best way to deepen your knowledge in the classroom. This is one of the lessons I gained during my internship at the Lagos University Teaching Hospital (LUTH).

At LUTH, I got to see how doctors were interacting with patients. I watched as they asked their patients about their health history: if they were on certain medications, if they had any health complications, if anyone in their families had a history of conditions such as diabetes, hypertension, etc. They would also ask what their living situation was like, if they had access to basic amenities like clean water, a place to sleep, and more. These questions reinforced the ways internal and external factors can impact a person's health and how providing care is more complex than simply prescribing drugs.

I had learned about genetics in my Biology classes and Social Determinants of Health in my Sociology classes, but I had not gotten to use that knowledge in this kind of setting.

My internship added a new level of practicality to what I was learning in school and gave me a new perspective on why I needed to pay attention in my classes and pursue academic excellence. It wasn't just about getting good grades. It was about making sure I fully understood all I was being taught so I could be a doctor who is "clinically excellent, culturally competent, and socially conscious," just like the Student National Medical Association's (SNMA) mission statement says.

I know that depending on where you live, the resources you have access to, and your academic interests, it might be challenging to find opportunities to utilize your learning in the classroom in practical ways. Trust me, there are more ways you can apply your knowledge than you realize.

If you are interested in becoming a physician, you could ask your school's clinic if there is any way you can help them out. If you know a doctor in your community, you can ask them if you can come in to observe how patients are checked in when they come to a hospital, and maybe even take notes for them. Do you want to go into journalism? You can join your school's news team or help create one if there is none. Practice writing news stories with the knowledge you are gaining in your classes and practice sharing them with people in and outside your school.

There are many examples I could give, but the list is inexhaustible. I encourage you to find creative ways to practice what you are learning in the classroom out in the real world, because it will help your learning stick even more.

Next, we will look at how you can maximize opportunities that come your way in college and even create them yourself when the need arises.

Please make your notes here:

CHAPTER 6

Maximizing opportunities

"You miss 100% of the shots you don't take."
—Wayne Gretzky

Growing up, I used to hear that an opportunity lost can never be regained. I don't know how accurate that is, but it made me sensitive to opportunities and motivated me to make the best use of whatever opportunities came my way.

An opportunity I seized was back in Nigeria when one of my older cousins, Bro Tobi, sent EducationUSA's 2019 Opportunity Funds Program to my eldest brother. My brother, in turn, encouraged me to jump at the chance to get closer to my dream of studying in the U.S. While applying, I didn't even know the full extent to which getting into EducationUSA would change my life, which is one of the reasons I am very attuned to opportunities and constantly encourage younger students to make the best use of opportunities around them.

I will be sharing some of the opportunities I utilized before and during my time at Bowdoin and the lessons I learned from them. I hope that by reading my experiences, you are inspired to be on the lookout for those that might be around you or those you might be missing.

One opportunity can change your life.

When I joined EducationUSA in August 2019, it was the beginning of my journey to coming to Bowdoin. I had applied for EducationUSA's 2019 Opportunity Fund Program (OFP), which was a scholarship for high-achieving low-income students where EducationUSA provided guidance and financial support for applying to study in the United States.

The program helped me understand the various colleges and universities present in the U.S., showed me how to apply to schools, paid for my SAT, and lent me books to study. It taught me how to research schools, provided me with resources to write the endless lists of essays, explained the financial aspect of studying in the U.S., prepared me to get my visa after I received my admission to Bowdoin, and gave me a proper orientation when I was about to come to the States.

It would surprise you to know that I almost did not apply to EducationUSA's OFP program. A few weeks before then, I had gotten into a one-day boot camp for young people who showed promise in change-making and social impact work. I had never attended anything like it before. It was where I first heard about creating my CV, the ways design thinking can help with social impact, and more. During the event, I met Victor Regal, a passionate change maker whom I would then go on to work with for two years, several months later.

After the Bootcamp, I was so struck by all I learned that I didn't think I needed to apply for the OFP. Frankly, I did not understand what I would get from the program, so I was not sure why I needed to apply. But before I decided not to go ahead, I spoke with one of my elder brothers, Joseph, and he told me, "Remember, one yes can change your life." That was what propelled me to craft my essays and put my very best into the application.

A few weeks later, I received a notification that I had been selected for the interview stage. I was ecstatic because by that point, I had learned a bit more about what I would gain through the program. There was only one problem: my interview date was the same day as my biology exam for my National Examination Council (NECO) examination. This is a national exam that most high school students in Nigeria write in addition to the West African Senior School Certificate Examination (WASSCE), a more internationally recognized examination. Since I had already written my WASSCE, my siblings advised that I go for my OFP interview, even though that meant forfeiting my NECO Biology paper. I had to make a choice, and I chose the OFP interview.

On the evening of July 12, 2019, while sitting in my mum's kiosk, watching the main road come alive with workers returning home, I received an email that read:

> ***"Dear Opportunity Funds Undergraduate Applicant,***
> ***I am pleased to inform you that out of 70 students interviewed for the Opportunity Funds Program (OFP), you were one of only 10 undergraduate students to be offered a conditional admission to participate in the 2019/2020 Lagos Opportunity Funds Program."***

You should have heard me scream for joy that night! I didn't know what to do other than tell my mum and call my siblings. I couldn't believe it. I was another step closer to becoming a full OFP scholar. Even as I type this, I can still see myself in my mum's shop, standing by the burglar-proof iron and thinking of how glad I was that I did not forfeit my interview because of my exam. Looking back, that was quite a risk to take, because what if I never became an OFP scholar? I guess we'll never know. For me, the reward was greater than the risk. I knew that that one yes could change my life, and oh, I didn't know a fraction of what that would mean.

Desires do come true.

I studied abroad in Germany twice during my time at Bowdoin, but unlike the typical way people study abroad, I went during my holidays both times. This was because, as a pre-med student studying Neuroscience, I didn't think I would be able to complete all my requirements in time. But this didn't stop me from going abroad.

From the end of my first semester at Bowdoin, I knew I wanted to travel to Germany. I remember sitting at my desk and watching the screen as my German-language Teaching Assistant spoke about the Christmas market. I thought it was so colorful and wondered what it would be like to travel to Germany to see them for myself. That would happen two years later, but before then, I would spend a rendezvous summer in Germany.

The first time I visited Germany was in the summer of 2022. I had spoken to my German pre-major advisor, Professor Klenner, about my interest in going abroad once we got back from the winter break. I can still remember how he told me, "We'll get you to Germany." Over three years have passed since then, and I'm so grateful I had Professor Klenner as my advisor and that he was just as interested as I was in my going abroad. Looking back, my decision to go abroad that summer was timely. It was the best thing I could have done that summer, because if I hadn't, I don't think I would have gone abroad at all during my time at Bowdoin.

That summer, I lived and studied in Hamburg. I took classes on the weekdays at the Goethe Institut while I traveled within and outside the city on the weekends. I made friends who were from all around the world. In my first class, there were over fifteen of us, and no two people were from the same country. Very cool, right? But I wasn't satisfied with just being there and learning, so I decided to volunteer somewhere. For the whole month of June, I kept asking people at my language school where I could volunteer, and it wasn't until the end of June that I finally got somewhere.

I learned of a one-day event for the Arbeiter-Samariter-Bund (ASB) and signed up to go even though I was barely conversational in German. I did so because I wanted to push myself outside my comfort zone and practice my German at a higher level. The day came, and I worked with German children of different ages. By the end of the event, I had grown more confident about asking for clarifications and interacting with native speakers.

Experiences like this are what made my first visit to Germany incredibly memorable.

You can seek opportunities.

On a Friday in November 2022, I visited Harvard Medical School (HMS) for the first time. I was a part of this community for first-generation and/or low-income students at Bowdoin called *Thrive,* and they had joined other schools that were bringing students for an information session at HMS. For those who don't know what first generation means, it is when neither of your parents has a college degree. So, although my siblings had gone to college, I was still first gen.

The moment we stepped into the seminar room and I received my name tag, I felt a renewed sense of inspiration for applying to keep pursuing my medical aspirations. I remember looking around the room to see all the HMS students that had joined us that morning and reminding myself that my dreams to attend a medical school like Harvard were indeed attainable. I, too, could one day sit in this same room and help guide the next generation of medical students.

After we visited HMS, I began to seek more opportunities to build community with other underrepresented premedical and medical students. I was particularly longing to meet other African or African-American students and physicians, because I knew they might be able to better understand the challenges I had and might have on my journey to becoming a physician. I asked a few people on campus about it, but I didn’t receive the responses I was looking for, so I began to ask people outside Bowdoin.

During Thanksgiving break, about two weeks later, I visited the home of one of my pastors. As I chatted with the other young adults who were there, munching on Nigerian pastries and getting ready to serve myself a tasty plate of Nigerian jollof rice, I got into a conversation with my pastor's daughter. At the time, she was a second-year student at Emory Medical School, and so I knew she would be a good resource to ask about finding a community of African or African-American students and physicians.

The moment I asked her about it, she stopped for a moment to think and then responded with, "You should check out AMEC." She went on to describe that this was a conference for underrepresented students and physicians that I would find valuable. I thanked her and made a note to look it up later that night. I just knew I had received a gem!

That night, I looked up AMEC and saw that it stood for Annual Medical Education Conference. AMEC is a conference organized by the Student National Medical Association (SNMA) that offers educational workshops and programs to help students and physicians with their professional development and personal growth.

I then became curious about what SNMA was, and upon further reading, I came across their mission statement, which reads:

> ***Student National Medical Association (SNMA) is committed to supporting current and future underrepresented minority medical students, addressing the needs of underserved communities, and increasing the number of clinically excellent, culturally competent, and socially conscious physicians.***

Yup, I had found my people!

Once I read about SNMA, I decided I was going to attend the next AMEC, which would be held in April, in Hartford, Connecticut. I wasn't sure how I was going to make it, but if you know me, you know I have a lot of grit, so I was going to get there one way or another.

You will have to seize opportunities.

"Opportunities are rarely offered, they're seized." You'll find that in *Lean In* by Sheryl Sandberg. I do believe that different opportunities come our way throughout our lives, but if we are not intentional about seizing them as they come, we stand the risk of missing a lot.

In the second semester of my second year at Bowdoin, I applied to get funding to attend a conference. This funding was part of an extra scholarship, called the Joshua L. Chamberlain Scholarship, which I received when I was admitted to Bowdoin. Up to that point, I had been intentional about using as many of the opportunities that came my way at Bowdoin.

Since I studied in Germany the summer after my first year, I already had a personal experience with spotting and maximizing opportunities. According to Bowdoin, the Chamberlain Scholarship is a $3,000 scholarship "awarded to a select group of students who have demonstrated academic achievement and have shown promise of exceptional success in college." We were to use the award to "pursue enrichment opportunities like research, independent study, career-related internships, and service learning or community engagement."

In my first year, I did not know what I would use my grant to do, but when I found SNMA in the first semester of my Sophomore year and decided I was going to attend the next AMEC, I had a lightbulb moment. It was this grant I used to attend AMEC in 2023 (and then 2024).

Both years, AMEC brought together over three thousand underrepresented pre-med students, medical students, and physicians for three days of impactful sessions, powerful networking, and community building. Here, I got the chance to meet with many medical students from various schools in the country. Seeing students with similar backgrounds and experiences to mine in several top schools like Harvard, Dartmouth, Yale, and the like was deeply inspiring. Not only that, everyone I connected with was open to offering guidance as I navigate my pre-med journey, which was so encouraging.

During my first year at AMEC in 2023, I had the pleasure of being able to moderate a session with six incredible physicians. The session, Married to Medicine, brought together three couples, all practicing physicians, to talk about their journeys and what being married to a partner in medicine was like. This moderation was impromptu because the main moderator couldn't make it that afternoon, but because I was volunteering at the conference, I was aware when this happened and immediately jumped into the occasion. I knew that to seize opportunities, I had to always stay ready, and my experiences at AMEC that year were a big reminder.

I was so overjoyed by all I got from AMEC that I applied to join the executive board for the 2023/2024 academic year. I gave an impromptu manifesto at the next executive board meeting, emphasizing how I knew what it was like to long for a community and then find one. After the election was conducted, I was selected as one of the two pre-medical representatives of the region and the youngest member of the board.

The next year, I again moderated two wonderful panel sessions, only this time, I had signed up to. This was particularly exciting for me as a student-podcaster because moderating sessions helped me utilize the skills I have garnered in the studio in other spaces.

I had medical students and physician-scientists as my panelists, and they joined me in discussing sessions titled "Everything I wish I knew as a premedical student" and "Becoming a Physician Scientist," respectively. Alongside moderating these sessions, I presented my first Global Health research poster titled "The Effect of Socioeconomic Status on Maternal & Infant Health Outcomes in Low-income Countries: A Systematic Review." This was my final project as an SNMA Global Health Fellow (more on this later), and researching maternal healthcare, a topic very dear to me, was such a rewarding experience.

In 2023, I attended my very first AMEC because I was looking for a community of medical students and physicians that felt like home. In 2024, I attended AMEC as a moderator, a research presenter, and an executive board member for my region. This was me seizing the opportunities I had sought out.

Although the Chamberlain scholarship was available to me, if I had not used it, it would not have meant anything. I still had to be intentional about making the best of the opportunity. And even when I attended AMEC, I had to make the conscious decision to seize whatever opportunities I was interested in as they came my way. Remember, an opportunity not utilized is an opportunity that cannot serve you. You will have to play your part in utilizing whatever you have or the opportunities that have been placed around you.

Smaller opportunities can open bigger doors.

In the chapter on friendships, I mentioned how I interned at the Lagos University Teaching Hospital (LUTH) the summer after my sophomore year. I had been longing for an opportunity to work in a healthcare setting in Nigeria for years, but when I travelled to the U.S. to start my studies, I did not know how it would happen. Then in my sophomore year, I learned about the internship grants my school had for students to use during their four years if we were working for an unpaid internship. I was immediately drawn to the possibility of working at home and began the process of searching for a hospital to work at. After weeks of reaching out to various people, sending letters, and having multiple phone calls, I was able to secure an internship at LUTH.

When I arrived home for my internship, I had conversations with people who were surprised I had chosen to come home instead of doing an internship in the U.S. As a student deeply passionate about accessible and quality healthcare for underserved communities, it broke my heart to hear well-meaning people suggest that it wasn't in my best interest to work at home, especially since Nigeria's struggling healthcare system is a core reason I wanted to become a physician in the first place. Yet, I embraced the entirety of my experience at home that summer because I knew that it was in line with my career goals. What I did not know was that it would deepen my perspective on public health and lead to my participating in a Global Health Fellowship.

After my internship at LUTH, I had a better understanding of the complexities of working as a doctor in Nigeria. Before that experience, I had mentioned being interested in public health and helping to build equitable healthcare systems. Being in the hospital, going on medical outreaches, and helping my department—the community Health Department—plan events, gave me hands-on experience I didn't know would set me apart when applying for bigger opportunities.

Because of my internship at LUTH, I was able to speak about my passion for quality healthcare and global health with a more nuanced perspective. In my senior year, a medical student at Harvard Medical School, Ephraim Oyetunji, whose journey has inspired me, said to me, "Many people speak about being interested in global health, but you have shown it with your experiences."

Utilizing opportunities requires hard work.

"Opportunities are usually disguised as hard work, so most people don't recognize them," said Ann Landers.

Interning at LUTH made me realize how interested I was in global health. As a result, I decided to apply for SNMA's Global Health Fellowship so I could keep deepening my knowledge in the field. At the end of the six-month fellowship, I made a LinkedIn post that captured a key lesson on opportunities and hard work that the fellowship taught me. The post read:

"There is a new certificate on my wall, but it is not there just because it looks pretty. It is there as my reminder that learning about things I am passionate about doesn't automatically make the experience easy.

When I got accepted to partake in the Student National Medical Association's Annual Global Health Fellowship in September last year, I did not realize how much time, attention, and energy it would require of me. From my classes to assignments, personal readings to our final research project, I had to put in the work to learn deeply.

There were many times I asked myself if I had made the right decision to undergo the fellowship, knowing I would have a demanding 3rd year at Bowdoin College, and oh, I wasn't even prepared for what was coming!

The certificate is on my wall because even on difficult days, I found the strength to keep learning, to stay engaged with the many aspects of Global Health, to do my work, and to remain curious. This experience reminded me that I am capable of doing hard work, and embracing the challenging aspects of learning is an important aspect of true growth.

Healthcare really has my heart, and if I were to choose my career path all over, I would still choose healthcare.

This milestone is a significant one for me, and I'm excited to continue learning, growing, and building.

There is a new certificate on my wall, but it is not there just because it looks pretty. It is there because I just received my first Global Health Certificateee!"

Yes, doing something I loved did not automatically make it

easier, and getting an opportunity will oftentimes require you to work hard. But don't let this discourage you. This hard work will increase your capacity and help you become a better version of yourself. Trust me, you will look back and be glad you did it.

After that summer, I started my first term as a premedical representative for SNMA Region VII, which was the region I fell under as a student in Maine. As a premed representative, I would attend several meetings every month, reach out to students in various schools in our region, help organize events, and assist with setting up new Minority Association of Premedical Students (MAPS) chapters for the region. This role required a significant amount of work each month, and as the school year went by, it became even more challenging to balance all my responsibilities.

This role was something I chose for myself, and when I decided to run for the position, I did not fully realize how much it would require of me. I had to constantly remind myself that the opportunities we get often come with hard work. When you hope and pray for something, you are consciously or unconsciously asking for the hard parts that come with it.

Don't rule out opportunities before you even get to try them.

Have I told you of how I nearly skipped Research at Bowdoin because I had assumed I would not like it? In my defense, I didn't have prior exposure to Research, and in my first and second years at Bowdoin, I used to get a lot of headaches from looking under the microscope for long periods. Turned out I was just looking into the microscope wrongly. I shouldn't have been looking in with my glasses. I figured this out in one of my labs (Neuropharmacology) in my junior year, and it marked the beginning of my journey to wet lab research.

From the beginning of my second year at Bowdoin, I had

concluded that I would not do Research because I didn't think I would like it. I was so serious about it that when I attended pre-med conferences or events, I would ask the medical students if I could still get into med school without Research experience.

However, they kept telling me not to rule out research without trying it out first. This was one of the main reasons I then decided to try out research the summer after my junior year. I was going to work in a neuroscience lab, working on locomotion research using the mouse spinal cord as a model for mammalian spinal cords. Since I had taken Neuropharmacology the semester before the summer I started my research, I became invested in the topic we were researching, which significantly impacted my experience that summer.

As a result of my experience doing research, I began to wonder how many other people rule out certain opportunities before they even get to try them. I learned many things during my research, but one important thing I learned was that access impacts interest.

This revelation was so important for me because I couldn't imagine what it would have been like if I had eventually graduated from Bowdoin without trying out lab research. I have always known that many students might not be reaching their full potential because of the communities they're in or the backgrounds they come from, so this experience reinforced that knowledge and made me even more eager to contribute to closing the disparity between students who have access and those who do not.

My experience that summer was what propelled me to apply, during the first semester of my senior year, for the annual summer "Project for Peace" grant, a national grant that awards $10,000 to selected students to carry out a peace-building project in a country of their choice.

About two weeks before the start of my final semester at Bowdoin, I received an email from Bowdoin saying I had been selected as their top candidate, and my grant proposal would be sent to the Project for

Peace Headquarters. In March 2025, I heard I had been selected for the award and would be able to carry on this project that was so dear to my heart. Had I not tried out research the summer before, I might not have understood that I had a role to play in increasing access to STEM education for students in underserved communities and schools, and this project might not have been born.

I encourage you again not to rule out opportunities based on assumptions. Simply assuming you will not like a certain path might lead to you missing out on life-changing opportunities and, like in the case of my Project for Peace, the chance to impact the lives of others.

If you have the opportunity to try something new, do it. Even if you find out you don't like it as much as you had expected or realize that the path is not for you, you have still gained a valuable lesson. Knowing what you like or would be happy pursuing long term is just as valuable as knowing what you do not like and would rather not spend years of your life pursuing as a career. Whatever the outcome, you will learn something, and that, in and of itself, is enough.

Over to you.

I cannot recommend specific opportunities for you to jump at because I do not know your immediate circumstances, but I can guide you through some questions that can serve as guides as you navigate finding, creating, and/or utilizing opportunities. Here they are:

- ***What opportunities do I already know of that are available to me?***
- ***What opportunities do I need but can't find?***
- ***Who are the people who might know where I can access the necessary resources I need?***

Please make your notes here:

CHAPTER 7

Leadership and its weight

"Leadership is practiced not so much in words as in attitude and in actions."

—Harold S. Geneen

A few weeks before the end of my final semester at Bowdoin, someone asked, "What are we going to do next year without you, Ruth?"

We were having our weekly Africa Alliance Board meeting, and someone brought up that I would be graduating soon, which caused the entire table to start speaking about what the next year would be like without me on the executive board.

I served as president of Africa Alliance, Bowdoin's African club, for two years in a row. The first time I served on the executive board, I served as a co-president, and the next time as president. Those two years stretched me beyond what I had anticipated. They were years full of growth, learning, challenges, discovery, mentorship, and more.

I can't write a book about my time in college without speaking about the importance of leadership and serving others.

Growing up, I heard a lot about how leadership is service, but that's honestly easier said than done. It's one thing to want all the accolades and recognition that come from being a leader of a club or organization, it is another thing to know that as a leader, you have to accept the wonderful and challenging parts that come with the role. You have been called to serve, to raise people who will feel confident to lead and can lead in your absence.

Truth is: it is not easy to serve. It often requires putting others first, and it can be challenging to do. We live in a very me-centered culture where we are constantly being told that we need to look after ourselves, sometimes at the expense of others. Self-care is crucial, but so is serving others. Through leadership and service, we become better versions of ourselves and help others become better people themselves. It's a gift that keeps on giving.

Throughout my time at Bowdoin. I was called to serve in different ways, and through all of these spaces, I've learned different things about myself and others.

At the start of my first year, I led an orientation trip for first-year students through Bowdoin's Mckeen Center for the Common Good. I also helped with coordinating Coffee Chats, a weekly one-on-one fellowship time for my intervarsity fellowship, JAMS. In my junior and senior years, I served as president of Africa Alliance, Bowdoin's African community. A leadership position I continued with from before college and throughout college was serving as a leader of Teennation, an NGO committed to youth empowerment and leadership. In July of 2022, I was appointed as Teennation's global president and have served in that capacity ever since. All these experiences have shaped my understanding of the importance of leadership—good leadership.

In my final year at Bowdoin, I felt even more led to serve than I did during the previous three years. This was particularly interesting for me because in those final two semesters, I thought I would barely have time for anything else. Yet, the call to serve and give my best to my communities felt more important than ever before.

Over the past four years, I have learned a great deal about leadership. While I am still processing some of these lessons, I know you will find them useful. Here are a few:

You can start from where you are.

In the summer after my first year, I was thinking of ways I could get involved in the Bowdoin community as a leader. I had already launched my podcast and was a leader at two of the organizations I was working at before coming to Bowdoin—Upsurge Global and Teennation—but I wanted to be more involved on campus. So, I scheduled a call with one of the staff members of the McKeen Center for the Common Good.

My initial interaction with this office was during my first week at Bowdoin when I went on a community service-based orientation trip (O-trip). I was drawn to the mission of the office to help students use their talents and passions for the benefit of society through public engagement. On the call with this staff member, I told her how I was hoping to get more involved with leadership on campus.

After a fruitful conversation, she mentioned that there was an available slot to be an O-trip leader, and I could apply if I was interested. This sounded like the perfect opportunity for me to get involved and contribute to helping other students have the wonderful experience I had the previous year. So right after the call, I applied.

A few days later, I was selected for the role. From then on, I went on to get involved on campus in many ways. Being an O-trip leader was a commitment that spanned only about two weeks, but it gave me just enough momentum to get involved in other positions.

I understand how it feels not to know where to start or how to get involved in leadership. It's easy to look at the big titles or roles and conclude that they are the only ways you can get involved as a leader, but this is not true. You can get involved in leadership right from where you are. Look around you and ask yourself the places and spaces you can get involved. If you can make a change, if you can help guide another person to achieve something, if your action inspires someone to be better, then you are a leader.

2. Leadership requires discipline and sacrifice.

Leadership comes at a cost. Many times, you will need to go the extra mile even when you can't see the way ahead. Leading various teams meant multiple meetings throughout the week, even when it wasn't convenient, stepping up to help someone with their task when they needed it, taking time out to offer guidance, and being disciplined with how I showed up as a leader.

Before every Africa Alliance meeting, I made sure to take time to prepare and send out the agenda. This required that I hold myself accountable to preparing adequately before any meeting, so that I could show up ready. When any of my teams had events coming up, I had to put in extra hours for preparations, checking in with speakers, performers, partners, or anyone involved, as well as coordinating with my team.

Every time Africa Alliance held an event, my board and I would spend time planning, setting up, facilitating the event, clearing up, and more. This meant that beyond the time for the event itself, we had to show up in several other ways. This was sometimes very challenging to do because we all had to factor in our academic and other commitments, yet we showed up as best as we could. This is what leadership often requires of you.

3. Leaders create the culture.

When I was preparing to lead Africa Alliance at the start of my senior year, I decided that all our executive board meetings would start with icebreaker questions. This is something I had learned from two other teams I had been on the previous year, and how I saw the teams' leaders set the culture.

As a leader, something I had to remember was that I set the culture that would be emulated and even upheld after I was gone. Creating a good structure is great, but creating a nurturing and empowering culture is just as important. Every step I took as a leader mattered, and the way I made people feel would define how they treated each other.

4. Great leaders raise other leaders.

One of my philosophies on leadership is using my light to ignite the light of others. A line from one of my favorite poems by Marianne Williamson says:

> ***And as we let our own light shine,***
> ***We unconsciously give other people the permission to do the same.***
> ***As we are liberated from our own fear,***
> ***Our presence automatically liberates others.***

Beyond doing great things myself, I knew it was just as important to help everyone I led become great leaders, too.

In the spring semester of my senior year, Africa Alliance hosted its biggest event in the whole four years I had been at Bowdoin. It was the 31st commemoration of the 1994 genocide against the Tutsi people in Rwanda. This event brought together Rwandan community members from across the state, students from Bowdoin and different colleges to reflect, learn, and enjoy community.

At the end of the event, we had filled up one of Bowdoin's main auditoriums like we had never done before, with around two hundred and fifty people in attendance.

Songa, Africa Alliance's treasurer during that academic year, was the officer who brought up the idea of having the event, and the rest of the board worked tirelessly to bring the event to life. Seeing so many African community members, many of whom travelled outside Bowdoin's locality, made me emotional.

As I listened to a phenomenal spoken word rendition by a student from another school, listened to the panel, and watched a touching documentary on how Rwanda has advanced since the tragic event, I held back tears. Bringing people in the community together was one of my big hopes for my time as president, and this event was a momentous one for me, the rest of the executive board, and the entire college. But this vision did not start out that big.

A year before this event was held, on May 1st, 2024, we held the 30th commemoration. We didn't think of the event early enough, so we barely did any planning. This also meant we didn't do much publicity. At that event, we only had eight people in attendance, including Songa and me. Still, it was such a beautifully intimate and successful event. At the end of the event, I texted the group saying: "Songa, you did an AMAZING job tonight! Thank you for hosting and for creating space for remembrance, learning, and conversation. We definitely should do more events like this next year," to which Songa replied, "We'll do it bigger next year." What neither of us knew at that moment was that it would not only be bigger, it would be a one-of-a-kind event.

So when a year later, we had a packed auditorium, my heart was full. As I chatted with Songa at the end of the event, he said, "Ruth, you don't know how much ambition you have given us as a board." I was glad to know that I didn't just keep my ambitious spirit to myself; I helped my board see what they could do before they even knew it.

5. You shouldn't try to do everything on your own.

As someone who likes things done a certain way, I have had to grow in the area of allowing others to do things their way so they can learn.

My first year at Bowdoin, I found it really hard to delegate tasks. I would assign a task to my team member and check in too often, instead of fully allowing them to carry out the task. As I grew as a leader, I realized that micromanaging my team was harmful for both the team and me. I needed to give my team members the space to learn and grow while I used that time to do other tasks I had at hand. By the end of my final year, I had learned a great deal about delegating tasks, which greatly helped me in getting more done in less time.

Balancing leadership and personal well-being.

Leadership often demands that you show up even when it is not convenient. This also means that there is a tendency to neglect your well-being for the sake of what your team needs. However, I have found that one of the best things you can do for your team and those you are serving is to take care of yourself. Remember: you cannot pour from an empty cup. So, taking care of yourself ensures that you are in the best space to be able to give to others.

During the break between the first and second semester of my third year at Bowdoin, I was on a call with a friend of mine when he asked what I was planning to do differently to help me better balance my responsibilities and take care of myself. I told him I was contemplating not applying to be Africa Alliance's president again the next year because I was feeling very anxious about the role. I was trying, but not succeeding, at balancing my leadership responsibility and my well-being, and I didn't think I could continue much longer.

Several months after telling Dulra this, I realized I was not feeling anxious just because of my role as a president; the entirety of my junior year was a challenging time for me for various reasons. Since junior year is the year most people study abroad, several of my friends were not on campus during one of the semesters, or even the whole year. I was also feeling very homesick because I had visited home for the first time in two years the summer before. This was all coupled with the fact that the campus felt tenser than the previous two years.

By reflecting on the reasons I wanted to serve Africa Alliance in the first place, and how there was much I hoped to achieve that I hadn't yet achieved, my drive was renewed. So, I decided to continue serving in my position as president, knowing that I had lessons under my belt that would serve me in the following year.

One thing that has helped me to balance leadership and personal well-being is delegating tasks. As Africa Alliance's president, there were key tasks I had to do, but there were many others I could delegate. Knowing when to delegate tasks was crucial in ensuring I was taking care of myself while leading.

Another thing that helped me was speaking to my close friends or other leaders whenever I felt very stressed by an occurrence connected to leadership. This helped me process what was happening and de-stress so that I would be able to handle the situation better.

Choosing collaboration over competition.

Throughout my time at Bowdoin, I saw the beauty of coming together for a common cause and how that was an avenue to pool resources and reach a wider variety of people.

Africa Alliance held different events with Bowdoin's Black Student Union, Student Organization for Caribbean Awareness, and other clubs. In my senior year, Africa Alliance decided to collaborate with another school in Maine to have an end-of-the-semester event. We chose to do this because we understood how much we could achieve if we worked together with the African club of another school.

While it is important to strive for collaboration, it is also equally important to note that not all collaborations will work out, and that's okay. After months of planning with the team from the other school for our end-of-semester event, we began to experience some tension during our meetings. I noticed that people were sounding more frustrated in their responses to each other, stopped communicating as well as they would before, and were becoming less enthusiastic about the event we were planning. After doing some digging, I realized it was because both teams were working at different paces, and it was causing a lot of friction.

About a month before the scheduled date of the event, we needed to make a decision—would we go ahead with the event that semester or push it to the next semester? Our team wanted to go ahead with the event that semester because we had already come a long way with planning, and thought pushing the event back a semester would not help much. However, the other team was set on moving the event to the next semester because they believed the planning was happening too quickly. Both my team and the other team had valid points, but both of them could not be the way forward; we had to make a decision. The stakes were high because if we couldn't agree on the same timeline, we would have to end the collaboration.

As president, I knew I had the duty of making a decision and communicating it in the best way possible. So what did I do? I prayed for wisdom. Yes, I prayed. Praying before taking leadership decisions is something I did my entire senior year, and it greatly impacted my leadership. After praying about the best way to approach the situation, I was led to go ahead with the event that semester. I knew our team was capable, and while the planning was happening a little too quickly, moving the event to the next semester would have greatly offset our calendar of events.

Once the rest of the Africa Alliance board and I decided to continue with the event that semester, I sent a long and thoughtful message to the other team. I made sure to explain that I understood why they wanted us to move the event. Yet, it would significantly impact our club's timeline. To my surprise, I got a very positive response from the other team.

Once we had agreed, we took our planning to the next level, sending all the necessary emails, checking in with all our performers, and more. At the end of the semester, we were able to host a memorable and successful event. As the event ended, I spotted the students we were working with from the other school. They had come to celebrate with us, affirming that both boards were on good terms.

Despite the issues we had with making this collaboration work, the success of the event reaffirmed that fostering collaborations is a vital part of leadership. Rather than striving to out-compete another club or assert dominance, working together can have tremendous benefits for you and the people you want to serve.

Leadership and its challenges.

There's a proverb I heard growing up that says, "Heavy is the head that wears the crown." This proverb is intriguing, and I want to point out two things from it. One: it acknowledges that the person is wearing a crown, and a crown is something to be desired. It looks pretty and attracts attention. This shows how the position of leadership has a level of prestige to it. It's something that can bring attention, praise, and make the person involved feel great about themselves. But the crown in this proverb also bears some weight that can become heavy for the wearer. Sometimes, the weight of the crown is manageable. Other times, it could feel crushing.

In my first semester as co-president of Africa Alliance, our executive board had to decide on sending out a statement to the whole club in response to a conflict that had ensued. This was an important and sensitive move because, as leaders, whatever statement we made would be seen as a reflection of our stance on the executive board and even the whole club. We had to find a way to communicate with the rest of the club and speak up, while still acknowledging the issue was very complex.

The weeks leading up to when we sent the statement were more emotionally demanding than I was prepared for. As leaders, we were also just students navigating this complex situation and the other things going on in our individual lives. So having the weight of speaking as representatives for the club was a tough one to bear.

In one particular executive board meeting, we had some members of the club join us in the meeting. They felt strongly about us making a statement and affirming one side. That encounter will stay with me for a long time. They came in airing their grievances, and they made good points. But the manner with which they communicated with us was more confrontational; they weren't exactly trying to understand the complex situation. They accused the board of being silent in a way that was unfair to the fact that we had been thinking the best way to go about the situation.

After the meeting, one of the members of our board wrote a draft of the statement and shared it with the rest of us. I knew the statement needed more mature eyes to look over it, but I wasn't sure how we would get that.

For many days, I prayed for help because I did not want us to send out a statement that did not properly encapsulate what we stood for as a board and the complexity of the matter. This was also the semester I was feeling very homesick, so combining that with homesickness and a host of other things was just so anxiety-inducing.

After about two weeks of back and forths about the statement, somebody on the board said she knew a professor who could come into one of our meetings to look at the statement. This was great news to me, because we needed the help in case there were any blind spots we were missing and inaccurate claims we were making. When the professor came, she pointed out important things.

That semester, I had many mornings when I would wake up with my chest heavy and tight. My days were filled with anxiety, and it was affecting my entire semester.

Conflicts in leadership.

Facing conflict in leadership is a normal occurrence. When you work with a group of people, there is a chance that things will come up where people have different opinions and approaches. This can then lead to strong feelings and conflicts of different scales.

During my time as a leader at Bowdoin, I had to partake in conflict resolution whenever the need arose. This was never easy to do because handling conflict is a delicate process, and handling it poorly can aggravate the situation. Conflicts are also emotionally taxing, so there were days when I felt distracted and overwhelmed because of a conflict I was trying to resolve.

After learning about conflict resolution and practicing it, here are a few lessons I learned about avoiding conflict and resolving it when it arises.

- Communication is key. Communication ensures that every party is on the same page, thereby reducing the effects of miscommunication. When a plan is made, it needs to be clearly communicated to the rest of the group, and if it happens to change, no one should be left in the dark. Since successful communication requires that all the parties involved are clear on what is being communicated, it is important not to assume where people are. And when conflict arises, it is important to communicate the cause of the conflict, what people's expectations were, and how best it can be resolved.

- Transparency is vital when working with a team and handling conflict. Don't make decisions behind people's backs or after a previous agreement has been made. Dishonesty or secrecy can sow discord in teams and can take months and years to repair.

- A third lesson is that showing respect to everyone you work with can help prevent unnecessary conflict. When conflicts arise, it is important to maintain respect for everyone involved. It is unprofessional, hurtful, and honestly just wrong to speak to a person disrespectfully because you don't agree with them or you would like to do something differently. I have learned that even for things that seem small, they can snowball into something bigger and hurtful to a person. A joke can start as a joke and then become offensive when it is repeated over and over.

- The final lesson is that conflicts always teach us something. Whether it is a conflict between two people or a conflict between an entire team, resolving a conflict is something that helps us become better leaders, friends, classmates, and people in general.

The reality is that the effects of conflict might sometimes be long-lasting. So, whenever conflict arises, we need to do our best to resolve it as best as we can. It's possible to avoid major conflicts when working with people, but even when they arise, know that it's simply a part of the leadership experience.

Moving on and letting go.

As I prepared to wrap up my time at Bowdoin, I had a conversation with SJ Tinker, one of the Residential Life staff members I worked closely with for two years, and she said something about leadership that struck me. She said leadership also meant "learning how to let go," and this felt timely. That semester, I would hand over various things in preparation for my transition out of Bowdoin, and I knew it wouldn't be easy. But learning to pass on my knowledge to the next generation of leaders was vital.

You will have to transition from one leadership role to another and will need to make space for other people to lead. Learning to allow others to take on the leadership roles you once held is a sign of maturity and humility—qualities every great leader needs to have.

Serving isn't just a thing you do if you feel like it; it's a way of life. I'm honored to have been able to serve in various capacities and hope you will take the chance you have to lead and serve.

Please make your notes here:

CHAPTER 8

Taking care of yourself

"Rest and self-care are so important. When you take time to replenish your spirit, it allows you to serve others from the overflow. You cannot serve from an empty vessel."

—Eleanor Brownn

I'm typing this at 12:50 a.m. on the second Thursday of my final semester at Bowdoin, somewhere in Smith Union, the main student activities building. I have just finished an assignment for my physics class that took me nearly five hours to complete because I had to ask a friend to explain some of the concepts I had not fully understood.

My body is tired, and my brain is begging for rest. This is the latest I've been out this week (which is even earlier than I go to bed on some days). I've tried hard to get better sleep this semester, and while only two weeks feels early to conclude, I've been doing a good job. Well, here I am telling you this at almost one a.m., but one slip-up doesn't flush all my progress down the drain, right?

I can't believe I'm writing about resting because it is a subject I struggled with for most of my time at Bowdoin. What's more ironic than a wellness podcaster struggling with getting rest? Sigh.

In my junior and senior years at Bowdoin, anytime I went for long periods without sleeping well, one of my very good friends, Alex, would joke about writing an op-ed when I became famous about how he knew me and my bad sleeping habits in college. I would laugh with him, and maybe even at myself for not fully taking my own advice in terms of getting rest, but I was not doing this intentionally.

My first year struggles with rest.

My first year was an especially challenging time for me in terms of resting. I was working hard in my classes, doing my on-campus job, being active with my extracurricular activities, trying to keep in touch with friends and family at home and abroad, all while adjusting to a new environment.

In my first year, I worked two types of night shifts. I didn't have to work at night in particular, but I chose to because I didn't want my work to interfere with my academics. The first one was a shift from nine p.m. to midnight, while the second one was a shift that went from ten p.m. to two a.m. In the first one, I would finish my shift, clock out, walk to my dorm a few minutes away, often yawning on the way, and still sit at my desk to study or do homework. I was usually very tired at that point, but because I struggled with allowing myself rest, I would sit at my desk, working, or at least attempting to work, for one, two, or sometimes even three hours. I never got much done because I was usually too tired to do quality work, but I still hardly went to bed right after work.

What I wish I knew was that the amount of work I was getting done most times was not worth how much sleep I was losing, or worth the effects of being sleep deprived that I would struggle with throughout the day. I remember how I experienced headaches in my classes and struggled with concentrating because of exhaustion. What an experience that was.

Looking back, I try to be mindful of how I speak of first-year me and her sleeping habits, because it was not easy to settle into another country as a seventeen-year-old, while balancing a host of other things. I also had high expectations for myself and knew people had the same, so I wanted to go the extra mile with my efforts. The expectations I had for myself contributed to why I found it hard to rest, and it has taken me years to learn how to find the balance. I'm still learning how to rest better, even as I type this, but I'm glad to be at a place where I better understand how important rest is for my body and my mind and the ways I show up to the world.

The importance of rest.

Have you noticed how irritable you sometimes are when you have not rested well? Or how you struggle with understanding things like you normally would? This is because rest is crucial for your overall well-being. Rest allows your body to recover, repair, and recharge, which leads to a better mood, improved energy levels, and so much more. When you are adequately rested, you are also able to do the things you love better. The difference is often clear. Here are a few important reasons you should rest.

1. Helps repair muscles:

Rest, especially sleep, plays an important role in helping you repair your muscles and in facilitating your growth. By allowing your body to recover after engaging in physical activities, you reduce your chances of getting injured and improve your performance. This is why having rest days is often recommended as part of your exercise regime and is an important part of staying active.

2. Reduces stress and anxiety:

Stress is a part of life, and it can come in different forms. During stress and anxiety, your body experiences fight or flight, an activation of your body's sympathetic nervous system. This activation is meant to help you respond to perceived threats, but it can also occur even when there are no immediate threats in sight.

When you are stressed, your body also releases a stress-related hormone—cortisol. While cortisol is not a bad hormone, too much of it can cause an increased heart rate, blood pressure, among other things.

Resting helps activate your parasympathetic nervous system, which is involved in prompting rest, increasing digestion, and decreasing your heart rate when necessary. Resting also helps reduce your cortisol levels and puts your body in a more balanced state.

3. Improves creativity and productivity:

When you are well-rested, your brain can better process information and act on it. Just like other muscles in your body, your brain works less when it is fatigued. Rest fosters creativity and allows your brain to better process tasks that you need to do. This is why people take time off, are intentional about resting at the end of the day, and the like. When you don't rest, you might spend two hours doing something that could have taken you an hour, and you might not even do it as well as you could.

Other important benefits of rest include better digestion, improved cardiovascular health, a stronger immune system, reduced inflammation, and more. The list is inexhaustible, and I hope you can see how rest serves you.

Something I always try to remind myself of is that rest is not a waste of time; it is an investment in time. So while you think you might be gaining more time by sleeping only five hours, or not getting rest when you know you could, you are shortchanging yourself.

It's worth noting that rest doesn't just mean sleeping. While sleeping is a way to rest, it is possible not to feel rested even after sleeping. Rest can also mean doing activities that help you feel rejuvenated, and this can vary from person to person.

So, how can you practice rest? I mention a few below, but I also want to add that activities that are restful can be subjective. Something that feels like rest to one person might be stress-inducing to another. So, it is important to find what works for you. This can make a huge difference in how you feel when you practice either the things outlined in this chapter or ones you have heard or read somewhere else.

Different ways to rest:

- ***Get quality sleep:***

I know this might sound obvious, but the simple nature of the concept of sleep is why many of us so often overlook it.

Getting quality sleep is a great way to rest and can help you gain many of the benefits outlined above. Many doctors recommend getting between seven to nine hours of sleep.

You can get quality sleep by having a regular sleep schedule, limiting your screen time before bed, and creating a conducive sleep environment for yourself.

- ***Practice journaling:***

Do you know that when you have a lot on your mind, it can hinder you from feeling rested even when you are trying to? This is why writing down your thoughts can be a way to give yourself some mental rest. I have even noticed that when many ideas or tasks are popping into my head while I'm attempting to sleep, I won't be able to sleep until I write them down. Journaling is an overall great practice.

- ***Take short breaks during the day:***

Breaks as small as five minutes can help you slow down and reorient yourself, which can lead to you feeling refreshed. This can help increase your energy levels, improve your mood, and boost your productivity.

- ***Set times when you'll be without your devices:***

For some of us, our devices have become a significant part of our lives. We use them at home, in school, at work, with friends, and many times even when we're resting. These devices often come with notifications that can be distracting and overstimulating, which can hinder your ability to rest. Spending time away from your screens can improve your mood and energy levels in significant ways.

- ***Spend some time outside:***

Whether you're going for a walk, just taking in some fresh air, or watching the sun set, being outside is a way to rest. I know that not everyone lives in communities that might be conducive for being outside or being able to go for a casual walk, so I hope that if this is your experience, you can find other things to do that are equally restful.

- ***Surround yourself with people you love:***

Have you noticed how you can have a conversation with someone you love and leave the room feeling rejuvenated and ready to take on the day or the rest of the week? Being around people you love can be refreshing and help you deal with stress.

Setting boundaries and saying "No."

"If your compassion does not include yourself, it is incomplete," said Jack Kornfield. This is important to speak about because protecting your personal space is an important part of taking care of yourself.

I know it can be hard to say no to certain people or requests, but respecting your own needs and ensuring that you are not stretching yourself thin will allow you to be the person you want to be, both for yourself and for others.

We all have limited time, energy, and resources. When you

constantly take on more than you can carry, you stand the chance of getting burned out, experiencing constant exhaustion, and not being able to give your best effort to your commitments. You might also start building resentment towards the people you struggle to say no to. You may even resent yourself. This is why setting boundaries is important both for your health and for nurturing healthy relationships.

This might look like not receiving calls at certain times of the day, setting limits on who comes into your personal space, putting a timer on certain apps on your phone, establishing limits on how you spend, etc. You might need to set boundaries with family, friends, colleagues, and other people in your life.

Know that setting boundaries can take time, so be patient with yourself and others so that you don't feel frustrated too early if things are not working out. When setting boundaries, it is also important to communicate clearly and not assume people will know what your boundaries are because they are close to you. It is only fair to others that they know what those boundaries are, so they are not crossing lines they didn't even know were present.

Self-care, selflessness, and selfishness.

When speaking about self-care, it is important to also speak about selflessness and selfishness.

Taking care of yourself does not equate to selfishness. According to the Merriam-Webster dictionary, selfishness is being excessively concerned with oneself. It is seeking your own advantage, well-being, or pleasure without regarding others. Self-care does not mean we have to neglect other people or do whatever we want, regardless of how it would impact those around us. Being considerate of others is important even when you are taking care of yourself. This is not to say that you should always do things to please others, but rather that your means of taking care of yourself should not harm others.

There are times when you might be asked to do something for someone else, which might negatively impact you in one way or another, and it is more than okay to say no. In some instances, it might even seem like your refusal might impact the other person, but that is not enough reason to engage in something that will harm you. However, it is also important to look out for the needs of others. This is where the topic of selflessness comes in.

Selflessness is defined by the Cambridge Dictionary as the quality of caring more about the needs and wants of others than about your own needs. Selflessness is interesting to think about in the context of self-care, because it almost feels like a contrast to all we have said earlier. However, the key here is *balance.*

It is important to look out for others and not be preoccupied with just your well-being, but it is just as important to take care of yourself. There's a thin line between being selfless and totally disregarding your needs, and it's crucial to be aware of when you are crossing that line, as it might negatively impact you in different ways. Eleanor Brownn's quote on how you cannot pour from an empty cup is a reminder that if we don't take care of ourselves, we won't even be able to show up for the people we want to support.

Striking the balance between self-care and selflessness is something you will constantly have to do as you go through college and beyond. It will also look and feel different throughout the different phases of your life, which means you will need to be constantly introspecting.
Now that we have spoken about self-care, let's speak about other ways you can take care of yourself.

How can you stay healthy physically?

Your physical health influences the ways you show up to the world and should not be neglected. Taking care of your physical health is an important part of your overall well-being. I noticed that the times I experienced a lot of physical discomfort or health issues impacted other parts of my life. It's easy to think that if you don't have any current health issues, then you don't need to actively look after your health, but that's not true. In fact, it is harmful to think so. This is why it is crucial to be intentional about your physical health. There are several ways you can do this.

- **Stay active:**

Getting physical activity every day will help your body function better and help you avoid healthcare conditions that might result from a lack of physical activity. In different seasons of my life at Bowdoin, I fluctuated between using the gym and working out in my room. My goal was to still be active even if I couldn't make it to my school's gym or felt like I did not have the time. I understand that not everyone has access to a gym, and I am a big supporter of at-home workouts because they can be much more accessible.

- **Get sleep:**

Remember all we said about this earlier? I cannot overemphasize the importance of sleep. It truly is an important part of your physical health.

- **Watch your nutrition:**

One of the biggest things I struggled with adjusting to when I arrived at Bowdoin was the food. Since almost everything was foreign, some days I struggled with being able to eat, and other days I struggled with determining just how much food was enough. But that discipline is something you must develop. When you're full, quit eating. And look out for the healthier food choices.

- **Stay hydrated:**

Your body needs to be hydrated to function properly. You don't have to wait till you're thirsty to drink water, although that is a good sign that you need to.

How can you stay healthy mentally?

Looking after your mental health is a vital part of taking care of yourself in college. If you are not in a good state of mind, you will find it difficult to be present, show up where needed, and fully experience your college years. You might also struggle to feel connected in your relationships, which can be detrimental to you. Here are a few tips to help you look after your mental health:

- ***Be a part of a community and build a support system:***

In the chapter on building community, I spoke about how important support systems are. Having someone to share your burden with can make all the difference.

The semester when I failed my first exam, I texted my immediate brother and then called him. I knew that I needed to speak with someone so that I would not go down a spiral of despair.

Throughout college, as winter approached and the days got darker quicker, I noticed how it was negatively impacting my mood. On days I struggled to get work done because of the cold, I would work in community, even if with just one other friend. Knowing that I was not alone was usually what I needed to push through many of my difficult days.

- ***Monitor your use of social media:***

It is no news that social media can negatively impact your health. This is why, for many years, I have tried to put structures in place to limit my use of social media. Some things I have done include removing my social media apps from my phone's home screen, setting timers on the apps, and/or turning off their notifications. I did all three for Instagram, Facebook, and WhatsApp. This has been one of the best decisions I have made to ensure I have a healthy relationship with social media.

- ***Utilize counselling:***

My first time going to counseling (which you might call therapy) was in the second semester of my sophomore year. A few days before that, I was on a call with an alum when she mentioned how helpful it was for her while she was a student. After hearing her speak about her experiences, I decided to try it myself. Although some of the sessions felt like they were no different from conversations I had with my close friends or my immediate elder brother, I still found it useful to be able to process my emotions with the help of a professional.

A few weeks later, I lost a member of my family. This was a difficult time for me, and having support from counseling helped in that season of grieving.

I know that counselling or therapy is not widely available. I also recognize that people have varying experiences with them. I encourage you to try them out if you have access and see if it is something that works for you.

There are various stress management strategies. It is worth investing your time finding what works best for you. For me, sharing what was bothering me with someone I trusted was a good way for me to de-stress. I also found journaling incredibly helpful, as it helped me process my emotions.

Preventing and recovering from burnout.

The major burnout experience I had in college was the winter break after my freshman year. I had continued the commitments I had during my gap years in college, forgetting that I did not have the same time I once did.

Throughout my freshman year, I remember staying awake until three a.m. to send emails and work on various documents. I remember staying up till 6 a.m. one day because a big event I had been planning for one of the organizations I worked with was fast approaching. Looking back, I realize that one of the reasons I struggled to rest my freshman year was how much I was juggling and the time zones I had to constantly switch between. This made it such that I could work around the clock, even when I was supposed to be resting. As this continued, I felt increasingly tired and anxious, and this inevitably led to my being burned out.

When you try to stretch yourself too thin, when you ignore your body's need for rest, you stand a high chance of experiencing burnout. This is why, after my freshman year, I became intentional about watching out for signs of burnout.

The reality is that it can be hard to tell when you are becoming burned out because you might just think you are feeling fatigue or stress from what you are engaged in at the moment. Yet, burnout can have a significant impact on your well-being and your relationships.

- To prevent burnout, I was intentional about delegating tasks where necessary. This was not as straightforward as it sounds, but I did my best to let other people on my teams do their parts.

- I also usually didn't do much work on Saturdays. I sometimes had meetings and worked on assignments, but for the most part, Saturdays were days when I stayed in bed longer and took things much slower than on the weekdays.

- Another thing that helped me prevent burnout was constantly speaking to my friends about things I was engaged in. This helped me process whether I was beginning to spread myself too thin.

There is no perfect strategy to recover from burnout because our bodies and minds are so different. This is why it is important to seek help if you are experiencing burnout or experience it in the future.

How I recovered from burnout:

A few tips that helped me recover from my experience of being burned out were taking time to rest, speaking about my experience with close friends, reflecting on the possible causes of the stress I was feeling, reevaluating how many activities I was involved in, and reminding myself of the things that mattered to me. There is no firm timeline for the recovery process, but with time and care, your body and mind will heal.

After spending these past four years at Bowdoin, I have learned that I will have to reflect on my wellness journey throughout my life, and so will you. Taking care of yourself is not something you do once and then never think about again. It is an ongoing process, one that will change based on what season you are in your life. Taking care of yourself is vital for you to thrive in and outside of college. I hope this chapter has helped you decide to prioritize your well-being as you navigate all you have to do.

Please make your notes here:

CHAPTER 9

Building new habits and staying accountable

"Habits are the compound interest of self-improvement."

—James Clear

Your habits play a huge role in your life, whether you're a student, a 9-to-5er, or a businessperson. Your habits determine whether you can get healthy and if you will stay healthy. Your habits determine just how good a grade you'll have. They determine if you'll be known as a person who keeps their word or the one who shirks responsibility.

A person is made up of their habits. A successful person is simply a person with an arsenal of good, sound habits that make for success. To succeed in college, you need to develop habits for success. This chapter shares insights on how you can learn new habits, maintain those you have, and unlearn bad ones.

Tips for building and maintaining healthy habits:

- ***Start small:***

Every time I return to the gym after a significant period of being away, I make sure to start with easy exercises so I don't injure myself by doing too much right away. When trying to build a new habit (or restarting an old one), it is important to start small and then increase your intensity as you go. This will give your body and mind the chance to adapt and prevent avoidable injuries and fatigue, which would dilute your motivation.

- ***Understand your motivation:***

"Intent impacts intentionality" is a powerful phrase Daniel Kang said during a Blooming Daily episode I recorded with him in October 2023. This statement has stayed with me since then because it is true that our intent for doing a thing does impact how much intentionality we will put into it.

If you are going to the gym just to post about it, you will show up with a different intentionality than if you were going because you truly want to stay healthy. Whenever you want to pick up a new habit, ask yourself what your intent is for what you are doing. This exercise will help you be honest about what your motivation for doing what you are doing is.

- ***Track your progress:***

Many times, it's hard to see the progress we make from day to day. You might not notice how much your endurance is improving every time you run, or you might not notice how many pages you have read over a week. So tracking your progress helps you look back and see how far you have come from when you started.

- ***Set realistic goals:***

Throughout my senior year, I decided I was going to read books as much as I could every day. My goal was to read at least one page a day. Just one page. I set this goal because of how busy I knew I would be and how daunting trying to read several pages would prove, especially if the book was not assigned for one of my courses.

Having the goal of just one page a day helped me on days when I was close to giving up on building my reading habit. It's easy to want to set ambitious goals when you are building a new habit, but it's important to set goals you know you can realistically work towards. Having realistic goals will enable you to feel less overwhelmed and more consistent.

- ***Focus on consistency over intensity:***

Several weeks during the semester, I found it hard to go to the gym because of how busy I got. In those weeks, I tended to fall off my workout routine because I forgot that I do not have to do an intensive session in the gym for it to count as a workout. Even my at-home workouts were just as great! So I constantly had to remind myself that being consistent, even if it meant doing a ten-minute workout every weekday, was better than just doing a one-hour session in the gym on the weekend.

- ***Make your surroundings work for you:***

When I wanted to stop using my phone right before bed and right after waking up, I decided to stop putting my phone by my bedside before going to bed at night. This simple act helped create some more distance between me and my phone, which I knew was necessary for my well-being.

Oftentimes, our surroundings can make it hard for us to build our intended habits or stop old ones. An act of changing even just one thing in your environment can be just what you need to start building that habit you have been meaning to.

- ***Reward yourself:***

At the start of my senior year, I decided I was going to take myself out once a month to reward myself for all my hard work that semester. This could be to a restaurant, a cafe, or just somewhere nice. I started well and took myself out to one of the Indian restaurants close to campus (because I love Indian food so much).

The next month, I didn't take myself out because I told myself I had already gone out for other events and celebrations. Then I told myself same thing the month after, and the months after, until the semester ended. By the time the second semester came around, I had forgotten I had planned to take myself out in the first place. This hesitation to reward myself is something I struggle with a lot.

But my point is this: when you're smashing the goals you set for yourself, take a moment to reward yourself!

- ***Be patient with yourself:***

Every time I start working out consistently after going on a break, I have to remind myself not to expect my body to do the same things it was doing before I took a break. It's easy to just want to get back into it, but being patient with yourself is key for building lasting habits. When you find yourself being too hard on yourself when building a new habit, ask yourself if you would treat someone you love that way. Oftentimes, we are more critical of ourselves than we are of others, so asking yourself this question can help you treat yourself better.

Many of the points I mentioned also work if you are trying to stop a bad habit. This will require you to also start small, set realistic goals, find support, make your surroundings work for you, be patient with yourself, and more. I encourage you to use these tips whether you are hoping to build good habits, have been struggling with stopping bad ones, or are in between.

The power of accountability.

- ***Scenario one:***

In the summer after my junior year, I decided I wanted to rebuild my reading habit. I had too many books in my room that I had not read because of how much work I usually have when school is in session, so I wanted to maximize my break to build back my momentum for reading.

At the start of the summer, I found it easy to incorporate my reading with my research. But as time went on, I realized I needed more accountability. So on the first of August, I texted one of my good friends, Victor Onuh, to ask him how his personal reading had been going that year. I told him I wanted to do an August Challenge for myself in hopes of building momentum for the school year that would start later that month.

Immediately I told him, he got on board. He told me he had slacked and also wanted to get back on track. Since our mutual intent and goals aligned well, I knew we would be perfect accountability partners.

We brainstormed different apps we could use to keep a streak, but I realized they might require more screen time than necessary. I didn't want to download an app like Snapchat just for the sake of keeping a streak. So, we decided that we would send each other daily updates with the number of pages we read that day. This was the start of our #AugustReadingChallenge. The goal was to read for at least five minutes a day. Just five minutes. Some days, those five minutes turned into twenty minutes. Other days, I struggled to reach those five minutes, but knowing I was accountable to someone helped me push through.

At the end of the summer, I was so proud of how much I had read. The reading challenge helped me finish two books—one I had started years ago, called Lean In by Sheryl Sandberg, and another I had picked up earlier that summer, called The Women of Easter by Liz Curtis Higgs. Between that first reading challenge and the end of my senior year, Victor and I did two more reading challenges: a #FebruaryReadingChallenge and a #LentReadingChallenge. These reading challenges have helped me get back on track or stay on track with reading books other than my assigned course readings, books that I have gotten so much value from.

- ***Scenario two:***

A few weeks into the final semester of my senior year, I reached out to Tomi to become my workout accountability partner.

I had tried to do this with a few other people starting in my

Sophomore year, but it just never worked out. So, I wanted to try again. I decided I would join Tomi to work out on Tuesday and Thursday mornings, before a neuroscience course we were taking together.

Having Tomi as an accountability partner helped me continue showing up to the gym with the same momentum I had built while I was preparing for the start of the school year. Working out with her, and sometimes a few others, brought a sense of community to our wellness journeys. And even when the semester became very hectic and I switched to working out in my room, I was glad to have spent the time I did working out with Tomi.

In summary, habits and accountability go hand in hand. To form a new habit or strengthen an existing habit, find people who share the same goals you do. They'll challenge you, encourage you, and go the mile with you.

Please make your notes here:

CHAPTER 10

Handling homesickness

"Maybe you had to leave in order to really miss a place; maybe you had to travel to figure out how beloved your starting point was."

— Jodi Picoult

During the first semester of my third year at Bowdoin, I felt the most homesick I had felt since moving to the United States.

It was the semester right after I visited home to intern at LUTH for the summer, my first time home in two years. Being at home was more grounding than I had expected, and that affected how my time at home felt. I spent time with my parents, and for the first time, my mum shared what it was like when she became pregnant with me after having five other children.

Hearing her share the struggles she faced added a new depth of appreciation for her motherhood and deepened my gratitude for how far I had come. I lived with Nwozors during my internship, and at that time, they had twins who were about four years old, so the house was always bursting with energy any time they were home.

Every day, I would come home from work, excited to see them, to hear how classes went, and to spend time playing with them. Outside my family, I spent time catching up with friends I hadn't seen in years, or some I hadn't even met in person at all. Did I mention I ate some core Nigerian dishes I had been craving since I got to the U.S.? Amala, Ofada rice, Moi-moi just hit differently when you're at home. Being back home made me realize how much I had missed my various communities at home, and so when it was time for me to return to the U.S., I struggled with the thought of leaving.

The night before I was to return to the U.S., August 13, 2023, I sat on the well in our backyard and cried for the first time in a long time. I was so overwhelmed by this sadness that I texted Kate Nicholson, one of my favorite staff members in the Office of Wellness at Bowdoin. My text read:

> ***I return to the U.S. tomorrow, and right now, as I pack, I feel 5 times more emotional than the first time I traveled to Bowdoin (which, for context, was my first time traveling out of the country, and also traveling ALONE). I'm crying hot tears, and I don't even know why. I'm going to miss home so much, and it is surprising me how the thought of leaving is making me this sad.***

Even without realizing it, this was both a testament to how much I enjoyed being at home and an indication of the homesickness that was to come in the weeks and months that would follow.

A friend told me that homesickness is connected with loneliness. At first, that sounded odd, but after thinking about it more and reflecting on how I was feeling, I realized she had a point. I noticed I felt the most homesick during the periods when I felt the loneliest and most isolated, but I did not realize this when I was just beginning to experience it. It took reflecting on those experiences and connecting the dots for me to understand what I was feeling and why.

The concept of homesickness being connected to loneliness makes sense. The first time I truly felt homesick was during my first semester at Bowdoin. Exams were ending, and my friends were leaving campus. I remember sitting at my desk in the corner of my room, the lamp illuminating my cherry wooden desk laden with books, stationery, and sheets of paper. As I worked on my final paper for my First Year Writing Seminar, my roommates were packing their items and preparing to leave campus for the winter break. Suddenly, I began to get emotional. I picked up my laptop and the papers I needed and headed down to the basement to continue my work.

Even while in the basement, I could not stop myself from thinking of the fact that people were leaving for home or other places, so I called my elder sister. It was about two a.m. her time, but she picked up the call, and the moment she did, I began to sob. I genuinely did not understand why I suddenly felt so sad, because I had not felt homesick the entire semester. So why was I crying after going a full semester without feeling homesick?

I realized it was because the friends who had made Bowdoin feel like home were leaving, which made me more aware of the fact that I wasn't going home to see my family. My sister tried to comfort me as best as she could, but there was only so much she could say from so far away. I eventually went to stay with my Nigerian host family a few days later, which helped me feel less homesick. But that experience showed me how much being in a community you love can feel like home away from home.

It is interesting to note that while I felt homesick at the end of my first semester because my friends were leaving, this was not the case for the times I felt homesick during my Junior year.

As I was writing this chapter, I came across a quote by Carl Jung that captured parts of how I felt in the moments that I was the most homesick. The quote reads:

"Loneliness does not come from having no people around, but from being unable to communicate the things that seem important to oneself, or from holding certain views others find inadmissible."

This hit home because the moments I felt homesick in my junior year, it was not because people were not around or we were on a break. Despite being surrounded by people, I felt like I couldn't speak about certain experiences that mattered to me, or didn't have people who understood the specific struggles of being an international African student.

I'm still trying to figure out why I felt this way the most in my junior year, but I believe a big reason was that I had just gone home. It seems a void had been opened that my community on campus couldn't quite fill.

It's okay, and even normal, to miss home, but it is also okay if you don't. We are all coming from different backgrounds and have had different experiences with our families, which might influence how you feel about being away from home. I recognize that the topic of homesickness might be emotional for you, depending on where you are at the moment, so I encourage you to take care of yourself in the best way you can as you read this.

I have found that a key way to handle homesickness is to find things that make you feel closer to home. Whether that means calling home at designated times, having regular check-ins with friends from home, joining cultural clubs, cooking meals that remind you of home, and sharing them with others.

Depending on how connected you are (or were) to home, you might deal with this differently. If homesickness is something you are struggling with, know that you are not alone. The first step to working around it is identifying how you feel. So if you've done that, good job. You're one step in the right direction!

Please make your notes here:

CHAPTER 11

Dealing with rejection, loss, and failure

"You don't realize it all the time, but some of life's roadblocks, detours, and rejections are answered prayers."

— Steve Maraboli

Rejections are inevitable.

I had two gap years before starting my college journey. Meaning that after high school, it took two years before I could gain admission into college. I must tell you why there were two years and not one or none.

Some people think it was because I was fifteen years old when I graduated from high school. Others think it was because of the COVID-19 pandemic in 2020. But the main reason wasn't either of those, although they were in the picture. The real reason is what I will call my first experience of *mass rejections.*

During my first gap year, which was between 2019 and 2020, I applied to about sixteen schools in the U.S. I was excited about the thought of going abroad and put my very best into it. I remember waking up at five a.m. many mornings to make it to EducationUSA before some of our events, crafting tens of essays, and preparing for the series of interviews I did that first year.

In January 2020, I submitted some of my last applications and began to wait expectantly for the good news. By then, I had received a rejection letter from one school, but I had gotten over it because I still had many schools I was waiting to hear back from. So, I waited eagerly, nervously. I waited.

Then other emails began to trickle in, and they were not what I was expecting. It went from one rejection to two, three, five, ten, fifteen, until I got the very last rejection letter.

Over fifteen times, I read:

"Dear Ruth,

After careful consideration, we regret to inform you that..."

Every time I read a new email, it felt like my dream to study in the U.S. was being taken away from me, little by little. I opened each admission email with apprehension, fearing I would see another no. I spoke with friends who were also applying to schools and received encouragement from my family, but it didn't take away the hurt of getting so many rejections. I questioned what I did wrong, if I would ever be able to get into a school abroad, and if my dreams to study in the U.S. would die. I cried. It felt like all my efforts had amounted to nothing, like the opportunity I had in EducationUSA was ending there, and I didn't want that. So I decided I wouldn't stop after a year; I had to try again.

So once I had gotten over the initial hit of all those rejections, I began to think of how I could improve as an applicant. I spoke to my EducationUSA advisor, and it was clear that I needed to use the remaining few months before the next admission season to strengthen the extracurricular activities that I was a part of and build depth in the activities I hoped to highlight when the time for my applications came.

Thus, I continued my advocacy against gender-based violence that I had gotten involved in during my senior secondary school days, and I continued volunteering with King Homes Charity, an NGO doing great work in increasing educational access to children from impoverished communities. That was also the period I launched Teen Health TV, which I spoke about in the chapter about chasing your dreams.

During that period, I continued to build my expertise in what I loved at the time—health and wellness and advocacy. I say "at the time" because I was still discovering my interests, but the *discovery* phase didn't stop me from getting involved. I knew that I had to show that I was putting effort into growing the interests I was already aware of.

The next few months, which were during the height of the COVID-19 pandemic, were a big growth period for me. I got the chance to explore my interests in a way I didn't while I was still in high school, and this helped me better articulate what I wanted my career path to be and why. I developed a deeper understanding of my power to impact the world from my own corner with the knowledge I had and the passion I possessed. I hosted multiple social-impact events and empowerment workshops as the Executive Assistant at Upsurge Global, participated in lots of advocacy online, deepened my public speaking skills, and grew more confident in speaking about my passions.

This led me to being featured on two state television channels, Lagos State Television and Ogun State Television, for my advocacy against gender based violence. Apart from the things I did with organizations, I honed my skills in other aspects like fashion designing, playing the violin, leading the choir in church, and more.

There is a lot I could say here about what I did, but the point is not to give you a list of my activities, it's to show you that I took the wave of rejections I received as a sign to keep growing, keep deepening my interest, to keep striving to become a better version of myself.

I have learned that sometimes, the rejections have nothing to do with our capacities. There just might not have been enough slots in that job position, not enough seats at that program you applied to, the reviewers might not have seen your potential, and so on. Other times, rejections are a sign that we have some more growing to do before we can reach the place we are aspiring to. Maybe you need to practice your public speaking skills more, maybe you need to spend more time honing your writing skills, maybe you haven't studied enough.

Rejections can be very hard. I have had different rejections in my life and understand how discouraging it can be, sucking up all of your motivation and making you question your goals and dreams. But I encourage you not to let rejections get the best of you.

Keep trying, keep putting out your best, keep seeking those opportunities.
Remember, one YES can change your life.

Failure is not final.

Henry Ford once said, "Failure is the opportunity to begin again more intelligently."

I completely failed the first Organic Chemistry Exam I wrote at Bowdoin. I would have said I got an F, but my professor didn't write any letter grade on the paper, just the number I got (which was below fifty). So maybe I can't fully claim to have received an F on that paper. Nonetheless, I know I failed the exam, and boy, did I cry.

No, I didn't cry when I saw my results; I cried a few seconds after I handed my exam sheet to my professor. Imagine me running from the lecture hall to the closest bathroom to bawl my eyes out. I sat in the toilet crying and trying so hard not to be too loud, because I didn't want the other people in the toilet to hear me sobbing or sniffling.

With how the whole exam went, I knew I wasn't going to pass. This wasn't because I didn't think I would do well on some of the ones I wrote, but because I had a significant number of questions I hadn't answered. Why did I have that many unanswered questions left? Well, there are two major answers.

One: I came to the exam hall on time—or so I thought. But it turned out I was *late.* This was the first time in my life that this would happen to me. The regular class was between eight a.m. to nine a.m. My professor didn't want to add extra time after nine a.m. because of those who might have classes right after, so he decided to add the extra time before and told us he recommended it. *Recommended.*

He said the exam was designed to be written in the fifty-five-minute class time block, so I thought I would be fine without the extra time. I couldn't have been more wrong.

When I got to the classroom about four minutes before the regular start of the exam, *everyone* had already started. I couldn't believe it. People had already started twenty minutes earlier. Twenty whole minutes! This was already a poor way to start the exam, and it didn't take me long to realize that.

The second reason I did poorly was that I had several unanswered questions left. I had thought that if I explained to my professor, he would give me the start time he gave others since I didn't have a class at nine a.m., but nope, he insisted that he could not give extra time after nine a.m. despite my explanation. I guess it's true when they say we don't always get things just because we deserve them. I didn't get the extra time, and there was nothing I could do about that.

That experience shook me, and the next time I had an exam for that class, I made sure to come on time. I knew that the extra thirty minutes at the start were not something to take lightly if I wanted to do well. How well did I do on that exam? Definitely better than the first, but not as good as I wanted. I still needed to manage my time better, and there were a few topics I realized I hadn't fully learned and needed to revise more.

My exam scores got increasingly better as the semester went on, and I ended up passing the class, but not with the grade I had hoped for at the beginning of the semester. Still, I was grateful for the growth. I took on the lessons with me from that semester to the next, and even though I was just as occupied as the previous semester, I had a better result, something I had hoped would happen.

In his book, Hidden Potentials, Adam Grant speaks a lot about how success is not about how much we have done as much as it is about how far we've traveled. Many times, we learn a great deal after we have encountered failure of some sort, and that can help us be better learners in the future. When I read this in the Fall semester of my junior year, it struck me because I could see it in my final Organic Chem grade. I did not end up getting an A in that class as I had hoped, but I learned and grew a lot. I had come a long way from where I started in that class.

I am constantly learning to see failure as a reminder that I have a lot to learn and there is always room for improvement. A statement Chimamanda Ngozi Adichie made during her speech to Harvard's graduating class of 2018 beautifully speaks to this. She said:

> ***"It is hard to tell ourselves the truth about our failures, our fragilities, our uncertainties. It is hard to tell ourselves that maybe, we haven't done the best that we can... and yet when we do, we are better off for it."***

Instead of denying our failures, acknowledging them and honestly assessing what went wrong can greatly increase our chances of doing better next time. A key thing here is to be honest with yourself about how you did. If you are in denial, you will hinder your growth and miss chances to do better.

Thinking of failure as a path in your journey to success will help you in navigating it when it happens. It will help you to ensure that instead of beating yourself up, you show yourself kindness and extend grace to yourself. Another line from Hidden Potential that I love a lot says:

> ***"Beating yourself up doesn't make you stronger—it leaves you bruised. Being kind to yourself isn't about ignoring your weaknesses. It's about giving yourself permission to learn from your disappointments. We grow by embracing our shortcomings, not by punishing them."***

This quote always reminds me that getting better is what matters, not doing things perfectly. The reality is that you can never be perfect and will always have ways to improve, so instead of focusing on how badly you did when you fall short of expectations, you can see it as a call to re-evaluate where you are.

Failure can feel very personal, but I want you to remember that just because you failed a test, a quiz, a paper, an interview, or the like, doesn't make you a failure. You are so much more than that, and you are capable of succeeding beyond your expectations. I hope you always remember this!

Loss is a part of life.

At one point or the other in life, we will all lose friends, family members, jobs, opportunities, or something else. It is inevitable.

When I started at Bowdoin, there was a particular friendship I was slowly losing that had been a core relationship for me during the last two years of high school. This person was someone with whom I had become close friends over the years, and our friendship meant so much to me. However, our communication began to drop drastically in the months leading up to the pandemic and in the height of it all.

This friend, I believe, had enrolled in a program without telling me, and had become more distant because of it. I would send messages and not get a response for weeks, and anytime I got a response, it would be vague responses about himself, and the texts would be tilted towards how I was doing. I didn't like this one-sided nature of things and tried to understand how he was doing and where he was, but I could not ignore the significant distance that had snuck into our friendship.

When I got admitted to Bowdoin, I wanted to immediately share the news with this friend, to celebrate, to remind him of how long I had been dreaming of this, but our distance had grown so much that I couldn't. I was slowly realizing that our friendship might never remain the same.

So, I reached out to talk about rekindling our relationship because I was feeling hurt and didn't want to lose the friendship. But I could tell the distance was becoming permanent.

As the months went by and I started college, I would reach out to check in, but nothing was changing. It was still the same vague answers and responses after several weeks. It was high time I allowed myself to move on. Our friendship was never going to be the same again.

I recount this experience of losing a dear relationship while also acknowledging that for some people, I might be the friend they feel they lost a relationship with. In someone else's story, I might be the friend who wasn't keeping in touch anymore, stopped responding to texts with the same energy, or began to give vague responses about how I was doing. If I could hold on to all my friendships, I would, but that's just not possible. I write this with mixed feelings, but I am learning to accept that loss is simply a part of life.

In times of loss, you might find it hard to keep your hopes alive, to move on, to start all over, but oftentimes it's those very things that can help us heal. This is not to say that the pain from the loss will be completely gone, but rather that even in the most devastating losses, hope can be found.

Tips for navigating hard times:

1. Allow yourself to grieve:

Know that it's okay to feel sad. Denying how you feel might work for a period, but it is only a short fix.

When an author gave a guest lecture at one of my English classes in my final semester in college, a student asked about how to deal with the rejections that come with pitching your writings to different news outlets or editors. One of the things the author recommended was to build a system where you allow yourself to mourn that rejection, so that you will be able to move on from it.

I once heard that if you lock up those emotions you are feeling, they might eventually burst open at an unexpected time and lead to worse outcomes than if you had honestly acknowledged what you are going through. So it's okay to feel sadness and grieve for a time.

2. Don't try to navigate hard times on your own:

When I started the job search process during the first semester of my senior year, I had thought I would only need to apply to a few places, and I would get an influx of acceptance letters. This was not the case. Rejection emails trickled in from several of the programs and positions I applied to, and the rejections hit me harder than I was expecting.

The very first response I got, which was for a fellowship I really wanted and had done four rounds of interviews for, I was put on their waiting list. I texted one of my brothers and another friend and told them how disappointed I was. I had hoped and prayed I would get that fellowship and had even begun imagining my life in that city, so finding out I didn't get in left me feeling downtrodden.

It helped to be able to let it out to others.

3. Find things that keep you grounded:

For me, one of those things is my Christian faith. Knowing that my future is secure in God is the biggest comfort I can get after every rejection, detour, or unexpected occurrence in my life. Apart from my faith, my close friends and my family have played key roles in reminding me who I am and how far I've come. This has helped me stay grounded even in the stormiest times in my life.

Finding the things that keep you grounded will go a long way in your life and help keep you standing when the rough winds of life blow your way.

Please make your notes here:

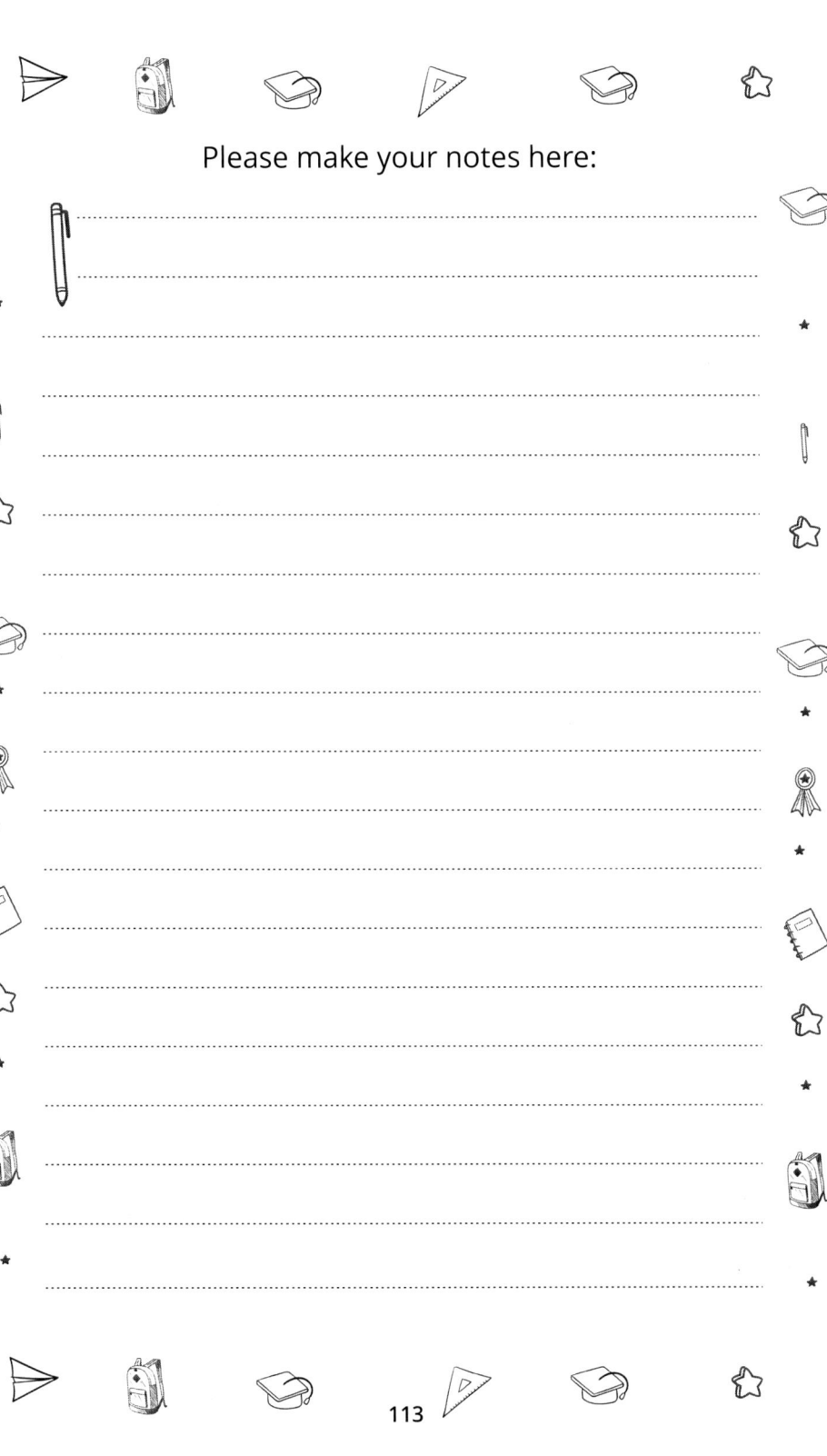

CHAPTER 12

Relationships and love life

"Love is patient, love is kind. It does not envy, it does not boast, it is not proud. It does not dishonor others, it is not self-seeking, it is not easily angered, it keeps no record of wrongs. Love does not delight in evil but rejoices with the truth. It always protects, always trusts, always hopes, always perseveres."

—I Corinthians 13: 4-7 (NIV)

I'm going to start by telling you that this chapter felt particularly challenging to write. There's just something about writing about my own experiences and lessons on love, at least the romantic type, that felt odd to do. Several times, I considered omitting this chapter because I wasn't sure how best to share my experiences. I didn't know where to start or what exactly to say, but the more I thought about it, the more the necessity to speak about this topic grew.

I knew I couldn't speak about lessons from my time in college without sharing the lessons I have learned about relationships and love. In this chapter, I'll share one particular experience with you and pull out lessons as we go. I hope that my journey of navigating that experience and the years that followed offers you valuable insights for your journey.

It can be messy.

The night I made up my mind to break off my first *situationship,* for the second time, was in November of my freshman year.

I was walking around campus with Juliette, who was then a senior, on that cold night as we spoke about something that had been on my mind for months. A few days prior, I had told her I was wrestling with a big decision and I wanted to get some of her advice, knowing she would have valuable things to share.

As we walked around the campus, I narrated to her how I found myself in a situationship a few weeks before I arrived at Bowdoin. I say found myself because that's honestly what it really was—I didn't intentionally choose to be there. I also didn't know how to define that relationship until much later, when I had gotten out of it. It was only then that I had learned what a situationship was: a romantic or emotional relationship that lacks a clear definition or commitment and often lacks clear labels, boundaries, or expectations.

I got into this situationship with someone I had been friends with for years. As you've read, I have a thing for long-distance friendships, and I love my friends a lot. I hadn't seen this friend in a few years, so some days before I left Nigeria for the U.S., we met to catch up and say goodbye in person, because we didn't know when we would next see each other.

As we sat in the huge shopping complex chatting about everything from work to school, big life goals to the new journey that was ahead of me, our conversation led to us speaking about relationships. We spoke about what being in a relationship meant for both of us, and as the conversation went on, we realized we both had feelings for each other. We had not mentioned this before because it had been so long since we saw each other, and being together in person intensified feelings we already had.

Once our feelings were out, the entire atmosphere of that outing changed. Now, we weren't just friends who were saying goodbye. We were friends who realized that being in a relationship was now on the table. We continued to speak about our friendship for the rest of the outing and what my trip to the U.S. might be like, but this time, with an air of continuity in our friendship, one that might lead to a relationship. I had not seen this coming, yet I was not totally surprised. Maybe because after knowing this person for the past few years and seeing how our friendship had grown, I knew that relationships could grow from friendships. I also liked him a lot, so the possibility of being in a relationship with him was inviting.

Things didn't turn out as I expected.

Later that evening, when we texted, I noticed that his tone and choice of words changed. They were more endearing in a way they had never been before, and that suggested we were now in a relationship. Mind you, he didn’t directly ask me out earlier that day; he simply expressed his feelings. But, because I had told him I felt the same way, he must have felt I was accepting being in a relationship with him.

That first evening, I didn’t know how to feel about the sudden change in our friendship status, but I also didn’t know what to do about it. Yes, I did have feelings for him, but that didn’t mean I was ready to be in a relationship. I was seventeen and more unfamiliar with navigating romantic relationships than I had realized. So when this whole situationship started, I didn’t know how to go about it, especially since I never explicitly agreed.

I knew, from that very first night, that something was off with, well, everything—the relationship and what it was trying to be, but I didn't fully have the words to express it. As a result, I limited my use of endearing words and would still be a bit taken off guard when I heard them. This made me think that maybe my hesitation was because this was a new experience for me, when it was, in fact, a discomfort with the whole *relationship.*

Several weeks later, I travelled to the U.S. to begin my college journey. We were still in this relationship, and I was adjusting to it, but I was still not fully comfortable. Although I didn’t know this then, I did not like how it wasn’t defined enough to speak to anybody about it. I couldn’t say that I was in a relationship, because I wasn’t, but I also felt a form of commitment to what we had.

As time went on and we began to have deeper conversations about love, marriage, and building a family, I noticed how different some of our core values about these things were. These included the place of our Christian faith in the family, something that is very important to me. The more we progressed in this situationship, the more I knew it was not going to work. Yet, the harder it was for me to get out of it. So, I stayed, but not for long.

The first week I was at my host family's home, I spoke to him very frequently, texting and calling almost every day. At the end of that first week, my host mum noticed there was someone I was always texting or speaking to, and she asked who it was. I told her it was just a friend from Nigeria, but I think she had a feeling it was more than that, so she advised me to tread carefully.

The next week, I decided to take time to pray and fast for the start of my time at Bowdoin. What I found at that time was that the unsettling feeling I had towards the relationship kept increasing, which I knew was indicating something important. At the start of that week, we had a call that led to us speaking on various things about relationships, and he made a passing comment about sex that I could not just ignore. As the youngest child in my family, with significantly older siblings, I had read different relationship (but mostly marriage) materials and had learned enough to be able to spot that our values were not aligning. I knew that if he could make this comment, then we must have other values on similar subjects that we would not be able to find a compromise on. And if there was any time to stop this relationship we had, it was now.

So, after lots of back-and-forth in my mind, I mustered the courage to call and tell him I couldn't continue with the relationship. I explained that I had not been comfortable the whole time and that our values were just too different. Our interactions over the past week of me being in the U.S. were taking too much from me and who I wanted to be. This was where I broke it off.

The days that followed were harder than I had expected. Since we had been speaking so much in the past few weeks, it was challenging to suddenly not have that companionship. I questioned my decision frequently and found myself overly explaining to him in the days that followed, trying to make him see that it wasn't about him but about my values and convictions. Looking back, I didn't have to explain myself as much as I did. I didn't have to make him completely understand, and it wasn't my job to help him heal.

A few months later, one thing led to another, and in a conversation we had, he remarked that I didn't care about him. In my attempt to defend how much I cared about him, we ended up speaking about how we both still had feelings for each other, even after breaking off what we had months ago. This was the beginning of the second round of the situationship. This second one did not last nearly as long, though, and it was while I was trying to decide on what to do that I had the walk with Juliette.

Making my decision.

As we walked, Juliette shared her convictions about her relationship with her boyfriend (and now husband) as a way to help me see what I had to do. As we spoke about love, she reminded me that I did not have to compromise my standards. She reaffirmed that there was no pressure to be in a relationship and that it was much more valuable to be single and thriving than being in a relationship, or in my case, a situationship, that was negatively impacting me.

"There is so much beauty in the single period," she said, sharing how the period of singleness was a great time for me to keep knowing myself, growing, exploring my interests, learning, and more. She reminded me that I had so much still in store for me and that if I confined myself to this relationship, I would be doing myself more harm than good; I would be hurting both present and future me. Did I want to keep struggling because of this relationship? Did I want to live with regrets about not getting out as soon as I could have? Did I want to lose out on a healthier relationship in the future because I chose to stay back? Those were questions I had to answer.

Since we were both Christians, she shared an analogy I have held onto since then. She told me that her desire for her relationship was that it would bring her closer to God. She said, "Think of a triangle. I am at one of the bottom corners, Jon is at the other, and God is at the top. Whenever we are closer to him, we become closer to each other, and when we are farther from him, we become farther from each other." Yes! I wanted that too, and could see that this was not the case with the person I was in this situation with.

Throughout this situationship, I didn't like that when I would pray, I would feel torn in the place of prayer. It felt like this relationship was serving as a wall between me and my faith. I had grown up to see God as a core component of Christian relationships and marriages, so being in this relationship I was sure God had *not* led me into was unsettling. I didn't like how I felt nervous, and maybe even ashamed, to tell God about it, because the more I was in this situationship, the more I knew I had to leave. The more Juliette and I spoke, the more I knew what I needed to do. There was only one option, and that was to end the relationship.

I don't know what relationship you are in right now, or if you're in any at all. Whatever the case, I want you to know that being in a relationship is not an accomplishment you would feel the pressure to achieve. I know mainstream media often paints romantic relationships as this thing to aspire to, but being single is more rewarding than we speak of. I want you to remember that you are still a whole and complete person without being in a relationship, and you can thrive while being single. In fact, you *should* thrive while being single.

So, if you are in a relationship you have been having second doubts about, if you know that you are in a situation you are not supposed to be in, please come out. I promise you will be just fine. You will not be starved of love, nor will you be incomplete. You have so much ahead of you, and I don't want you to negatively impact your future because of the actions of your present. It's not worth it—not a single bit.

Friendships can be just as satisfying.

As we came to the end of our walk around campus that evening, Juliette reminded me of the values of friendships and how they hold the capacity to be just as fulfilling. She said, "I hope that during your time at Bowdoin, you experience the deepest and satisfying love in your friendships. The type that makes you content with not being in a relationship."

Those words were one of the best things I could have heard at that time because I was just starting at Bowdoin and had about three and a half years from then to deepen my exciting friendships and build more meaningful ones while at Bowdoin. As I hugged her goodnight, I felt a wave of relief. Although I already knew what I had to do before our walk, I still needed to hear someone remind me why taking that step was necessary. That final confirmation from someone I knew had my best interest at heart gave me the courage to take that step, and I will forever be grateful that I did.

That night, I decided I was going to end that situationship for the final time. As I got back into my room, I called this person and told him, with the confidence I did not have the first time, that I didn't want to continue in that relationship. Telling him my decisions wasn't nearly as hard as it was the first time.

I cannot begin to explain the amount of peace I felt once I ended the call. I was filled with so much relief. It felt like I had let go of a heavy burden I had been holding on to for too long, and if I had held on any longer, it might have crushed me.

Instead of being trapped in this relationship, I wanted to cultivate the kind of friendships Juliette spoke about, the kind where I could shower them love without reservation and receive that kind of love. True love didn't belong only to those in romantic relationships, and I was determined to nurture those types of friendships and relationships with even my family members.

I did, in fact, go on to experience that kind of love in my friendships throughout my time at Bowdoin. I spent time deepening my friendships and cultivating friendships that were grounding, wholesome, refining, and constantly reminded me how loved I am. The more I experienced this love, the more I understood what Juliette meant, and the more I wanted to invest in my friendships.

Every year on my birthday, my friends have celebrated with me in the sweetest ways, writing the most thoughtful letters that hold such heartwarming messages. As I write this, I have tens of letters from my friends placed nicely in a packet called Treasure Chest. These letters are from my birthdays, and other big and small occasions I have celebrated throughout my time at Bowdoin. I have sticky notes with messages from my first and second year roommates, the type of notes that would make your day when you read them. Not only have I felt this deep-seated love in my friendships at Bowdoin, but I have also felt it in my friendships across the U.S., at home, and in other parts of the world.

I love my friends with all my heart, and I think friendships are one of the best things in the world. In the chapter on friendships and community, I spoke highly about my friends because that is really how I feel about them. If I could, I would pour every bit of love I can on them because they mean so much to me.

A few weeks before writing this chapter, I was on a call with a close friend, and after about an hour of catching up, we got to speaking about relationships. I told him that with the depth with which I love my friends and all the love I have experienced, I could only imagine the intensity with which I would love and care for whoever would become my spouse. This is one of the reasons I have continued to build depth in my friendships and channel all the love I have towards them, rather than worry about not being in a relationship.

My friendships have proven to be more fulfilling than I could ever imagine and have taught me a lot about love, trust, selflessness, sacrifice, commitment, intentionality, and more, some of which I spoke about in the chapter about friendships and community.

Mainstream media sometimes paints romantic relationships as the only relationships where you can feel an outpouring of love, but that is not the case. Just like Juliette said, you can have beautiful friendships that fill you up so much that you don't feel an unhealthy urge to be in a romantic relationship.

I desire to experience love in a romantic relationship to its fullest when the time is right. Yet, I am aware that romantic relationships are not the only places to channel and/or find love. Realizing this can do us better than we realize.

As I wrap up recounting this experience, it is important to be aware when the lines between just being friends with a person and being in a relationship with them start to become blurry. This is often what causes people to be in situationships. There are no defined boundaries, labels, or commitments in these kinds of relationships. You suddenly are in the awkward position of being more than just friends but not being in a relationship. It can be tricky to spot, especially since we can't assume what the other person is thinking or feeling. But if you ever do feel like you are in a situationship, then it's an indicator that you might need to be reflecting on that friendship and what it really is.

Your feelings are natural.

Throughout my time in college, I developed feelings for a few people and had people express their interest in being in a relationship. But the solid friendships I had formed helped me not feel the need to immediately jump into a relationship. I could speak to people anytime I noticed I was developing feelings for a person, and they would give me valuable and practical advice about those feelings. I did this because I wanted to make sure I was guarding my heart in the best way I could. Those conversations helped me re-center myself whenever I was in the heat of those emotions and made sure I avoided taking steps that would hurt me or that I would regret later.

One valuable piece of advice Juliette shared with me was that whenever she began to have feelings for someone, she would pray about it. She told me that instead of trying to ignore her feelings, she would be honest about them with God and ask him to help her control them. I loved this advice a lot, because it affirmed that my feelings were very normal and I didn't need to shy away from them. Instead, I needed to be open with myself about what they meant and what I could do about them.

So, throughout my years at Bowdoin, I would pray about whatever feelings I was developing towards a guy, along with talking about those feelings with people I trusted. I would pray that if I were developing feelings for someone who was simply meant to be a good friend, then I wanted my feelings for them to be clearly platonic, but if I was meant to consider a future with that person, then I should feel an inner peace and confirmation from God. This prayer is something that has greatly helped me, and I hope it helps you too.

Having feelings for a person is normal and not something you need to be ashamed of or afraid of. It's part of the process of growing up, and you stand a high chance of developing feelings for one or more people during your time in college. This is why it is important to have people you can share your feelings with when those feelings arise, so they can help you properly process them. They will also help you identify your blind spots and ensure you are not getting into a wrong or harmful relationship.

If you feel like you're feeling a lot of pressure to be in a romantic relationship, I encourage you to reevaluate the kinds of content you are feeding on, who your friends are, and if they are contributing to this pressure.

Love is such a beautiful thing, and I have experienced it in many forms. From being unconditionally loved by God to being deeply loved by my family and friends, I know what true love feels like. Yet, I am fully aware that this is not everyone's experience, and I'm sharing my deepest sympathy with you if you have or currently struggle with feeling unloved. I promise you that you are loved, more than you know it, and if you haven't heard that recently, I am saying that to you now: you are loved, always have been, and always will be!

Please make your notes here:

CHAPTER 13

Embracing your identity and loving yourself

"How you love yourself is how you teach others to love you."

— Rupi Kaur

Do you know that if you don't love yourself, you might find it difficult to show and receive love? You might have heard a variety of messages about self-love and might even be tired of hearing it all over social media. You might have also heard a lot about how to cultivate it, but depending on your background, if you've experienced abuse, if you were loved growing up, this subject might elicit a range of emotions for you. Whatever category you fall under, I encourage you to reflect on what this subject means for you and read along at a pace that works best for you.

Simply put, self-love is the state of having regard, compassion, and appreciation for *yourself.* It is an important part of our well-being and how we show up to the world. It influences us in different ways.

Now, I need to mention that self-love is not narcissism, which is more self-centered and is an inflated sense of self-importance, often characterized by arrogance. Self-love involves knowing that you, *too,* are deserving of your own appreciation, care, and compassion. It involves having a good understanding of who you are, your strengths and weaknesses, your flaws, abilities, and so on.

Multiple benefits of self-love are critical for your health. Self-love can lead to lower anxiety and depression, higher resilience, more motivation, better physical and mental health, healthier relationships, and even an improved immune system. So, self-love is not just a buzzword; it is important to pay attention to.

You may be surprised to know that when you struggle with loving yourself, it comes through in the way you interact with people. You might find yourself constantly making negative remarks about yourself, sometimes disguised as jokes. You might notice that you have difficulty accepting compliments; you struggle with saying "No" even when it is clear that you need to; you are always over-apologizing, and you engage in excessive people-pleasing behavior. You might also notice that you constantly compare yourself to others, battling with the feeling of unworthiness, and you might not take care of your physical appearance as you should.

This list is inexhaustible, and the fact that you're experiencing one or two things on this list doesn't mean that you don't love yourself, but it is helpful to keep them in mind.

What are ways you can practice more self-love?

Here are a few tips you might find helpful:

1. Invest in yourself:

One good way to practice self-love is to invest in yourself. This could be taking yourself out; enrolling for that new course; getting that tool you've been needing for a while, etc. There is no one way to invest in yourself; it depends on who you are and where you are at the moment.

Another way is being intentional about what you say about yourself. If you are someone who is used to speaking negatively about yourself, incorporating more nurturing language in your life can go a long way and is a great strategy for enhancing self-love.

2. Surround yourself with the right people:

Another great way to practice self-love is to surround yourself with people who see your potential, people who will cheer you on, offer guidance, and help you see when you are holding back from being the best you can be.

3. Extend grace to yourself:

An important tip is to embrace self-compassion. This means treating yourself with the same kindness you would offer a friend or family member who is going through a hard time.

For many people, it is easier to extend grace to other people than it is to extend it to ourselves, so practicing self-compassion can help challenge negative self-talk and remind you that you are deserving of kindness and care.

4. Set healthy boundaries:

Establishing healthy boundaries is also a great way to practice self-love. Boundaries can help protect your space and well-being and are a crucial part of creating a space where you can thrive.

In the previous chapter, we spoke about how important it is to know that you don't have to be in a relationship to feel whole. When you love and respect yourself, you will be more aware of relationships, both romantic and unromantic, that are helping or hurting you. You will also be more likely to leave when you discover you are in a relationship you shouldn't be in, because you will extend the same kind of regard you would to a friend if you found out they were in an unhealthy relationship.

The way you treat yourself will show people what you accept, and if you are with a person who wants to take advantage of you, you might be especially vulnerable. Nurturing self-love will help you focus on becoming a better version of yourself, a better friend, sibling, classmate, and the like, and help you overcome the desperation of being in a romantic relationship.

Enjoying your own company.

Over the last four years, I have learned how important it is to be comfortable in my own company. I need to be not just comfortable, but to enjoy my own company.

When I studied in Germany in the summer of my first year, I solo-travelled like I had never done before. While I loved all the times I traveled with friends, I also enjoyed the experiences I had on my own just as much. I know that I could not limit the experiences I had to only when I was with other people. Instead, I went to theaters, museums, and other places on my own. I even took an overnight train to Amsterdam on a Friday night on my own, which turned out to be an incredible and nerve-wracking experience. Imagine eighteen-year-old Ruth at a strange train station in the Netherlands at two a.m. I still had an incredible time, though!

In my first two years at Bowdoin, I lived with roommates. I enjoyed having that community around me and valued being able to share experiences with them. In my junior and senior years, however, I lived on my own in what we called a single because I was a proctor.

I have always enjoyed my own company, and those years deepened this. Living alone meant I had to be intentional about inviting my friends into my space or asking to come into their own spaces.

It's easy to equate being alone with loneliness, but that is not true. In fact, you can be lonely even while with people. Spending time alone is important to help you stay grounded. It also allows you to hear your own voice, which is even more important now when we have so many voices in our ears.

Body image.

Body image is a sensitive topic to speak on and even harder to write about. One day, I had a conversation with a friend, Funke, and she spoke about how she always reminded herself that her beauty is not attached to her body, but rather to the fact that she is made in the image of God. I loved this so much!

I am not someone who is obsessed with my body image, but I have had several times when I became too fixated on the marks on my skin, or how my face looked, how much weight I was gaining, and similar things.

Monitoring how our bodies are changing is a natural response to growth, but it becomes harmful when we start obsessing about how we look. This can harm us in more ways than we realize.

Loving my body in its entirety is something I am constantly reminding myself to do. Loving your body doesn't mean indulging in whatever you like. Instead, it means taking care of your body to the best that you can, nurturing yourself, and accepting your body's imperfections.

To be myself or to blend?

I'm a fan of long captions and reflective posts, and if you follow me on any social media platform, you will notice my posts are often like this. This is something I started doing on Facebook when I began to follow thought leaders who always wrote lengthy and captivating posts. Due to the kinds of people I followed online, seeing long captions and posts that had calls to action was the norm for me. So when I opened an Instagram account in 2020, this was how I built my presence in that space. Fast forward to when I arrived at Bowdoin in August 2021 and connected with schoolmates on Instagram. When we had orientation and the first few events, I noticed how short people's captions were. I wasn't sure if it was a cultural or just a college thing, but I noticed I began to feel very self-conscious about my long and often influencer-like captions, like my friends would tease me.

For weeks, I wrestled with how I wanted to present myself online in this new chapter of my life. I could choose to change how I showed up on Instagram, cut down my long captions, stop posting my reflective posts, and change my voice to fit what I was seeing around me. But that would just not be me. I would have simply been covering my light. I had to get comfortable showing up around campus and online in a way that felt authentic to me and ensured I was not dimming my light just to fit in.

Your dilemma may have nothing to do with social media captions, but you get my drift. If you're in between staying true to yourself, your passion, your voice, and your sound ideals, or going along with others, think about how much your voice means to you and what you'll be giving up for not being yourself.

Owning your identity.

In the spring semester of my senior year, I was speaking with a few first-year students when the conversation about accents came up. They spoke about how their accents were a part of their identities that they were learning to embrace in this new college environment. They spoke about how challenging it can be to embrace certain parts of your identity, especially when it makes it clear that you are a foreigner. This is something I could relate to, because many parts make up my identity and how I am perceived by people.

In college, you will constantly be in spaces that will cause you to identify as one thing or another. Learning that what makes you different doesn't make you any less is crucial for the way you show up in those spaces.

Please make your notes here:

CHAPTER 14

Navigating the Fear of Missing Out (FOMO)

"Fear of missing out is the enemy of valuing your own time."

—Andrew Yang

Would you believe it if I told you that I never attended a major college party at Bowdoin? The only parties I attended were birthday parties, and parties of friends celebrating milestones, which are different from the usual college loud-music, DJ-present, lots-of-dancing parties. The only party of that kind I ever attended was the MIT African Students' Association's 2025 Annual Cultural Night. I was there to support their president at the time, my incredible friend, Victory Yinka-Banjo. And after the main event, I stayed for the after-party.

Something only a very few people know about me is that I love to dance. It's one of my favorite forms of getting energized, staying fit, and even worshipping. I love how I always feel better after a good dance session in my room or at the gym (when there is almost no one else there), and this has been one of my biggest de-stressors at Bowdoin. So, you might wonder why I never went to a party at Bowdoin.

The thing is: I could already tell in the first few days at Bowdoin that the songs at parties would not be my kind of songs. As someone who is intentional about the lyrics of the songs she listens to, I knew it would be hard for me to control what was being played if I were at a regular party. So, I decided that rather than dancing in a setting where I can't control what I listen to, I'd create a space where I could feel completely comfortable dancing and screaming out the lyrics. There was no point being in a space where I couldn't fully be myself.

Funny thing is: I almost can't believe I made it throughout my time at Bowdoin without attending any parties as president of Africa Alliance for two years. Being president of a cultural group meant I was on the board when parties were being organized for our club members or when we were invited to collaborate in hosting parties. Even then, I still didn't attend any. I had made a commitment.

So, how was it possible for me to do this? There are different reasons, but the first thing that comes to my mind is my conviction.

A few days before I started college, I went to a college event organized by the Boston branch of my home church. This event was put together for incoming college freshmen and sophomores and was meant to help us prepare for the years ahead. During one of the panel sessions, one of the speakers who had recently graduated mentioned how she didn't attend any parties and how it didn't take away from her overall college experience. I found that interesting and decided to try it out in my first year.

About a week or two into my first semester, there was a party-like event held close to my dorm. It was out in the open, under a tent, and there were food trucks for people to grab snacks. I went with a few of my friends, chatted for a bit while dancing (or at least, attempting to), but I didn't enjoy socializing that way. For one, I wasn't familiar with most of the music, so I could barely dance to it, and then I wasn't used to chatting with people in that kind of condition. I also don't drink, so that's something that doesn't appeal to me at events.

In the first few months of my freshman year, there were various invitations to parties to socialize and build our circles, and I would sometimes consider attending, but my conviction held me back from attending. I didn't feel comfortable going and didn't want to end up regretting my actions, so I found other things to do and ways to have fun. This leads to the second reason I didn't attend any parties: I found alternatives that I was satisfied with. One of the alternatives was having my own dance sessions in my room by myself or with a friend. Being fully in control of the music and setting was something I enjoyed. That way, I could dance as much as I wanted to songs that still edified me.

Another alternative was something that was provided to me and other first-year students by Bowdoin. At Bowdoin, we have what we call *Duty Nights,* when a member of the Residential Life staff will be in the common room of every first-year dorm from nine p.m. to two a.m. on Fridays and Saturdays. Oftentimes, they would stream movies, have snacks, do karaoke, play games, or even just provide a chill space for people to meet and socialize before heading to bed.

I was at one almost every weekend if I was on campus, and I would chat with whoever was on duty. On weekends when I didn't feel like stopping by at Duty Night, I would watch movies in my room, chat with my roommate, get work done, or just rest. This was usually enough for me on a Friday or Saturday night.

The third reason I was able to go through my time at Bowdoin without attending college parties is that the more I didn't attend them, the easier it got for me to keep my commitment. I know many people found them fun, but since I hadn't used parties as my definition of fun, I felt less FOMO as the months and years went by. Looking back, I'm grateful that I stood by my commitment.

I'm not writing this to tell you not to attend parties or to make you feel bad if you currently do. Instead, I'm writing this to help you understand that it is possible to make a commitment and stick to it even when you might be feeling a lot of FOMO. While I did not party, I attended concerts and a host of other fun events with my friends. I found many ways to have fun, and I know you can too, even if it's not in the way everyone is doing it.

Peer pressure is real, but so is your ability to make choices and stand by them. Oftentimes, people will respect your choices if you are not imposing them on them or doing something detrimental to yourself or others. And the more you stand by your choice, the more empowered you feel to continue.

Sources of FOMO:

So, what are some of the other places where we often feel FOMO? I have listed a few below, but the list goes on. I encourage you to take time to reflect on the places you are feeling the most FOMO and why.

1. Social media:

Social media has made it such that we can keep tabs on how people in our lives are doing. This comes with its pros and cons. Advantages are that we can keep in touch with people both near and far. With a single click, we can share in the memories of people in our lives, and we can follow people on their journeys. But social media is also a huge proponent of FOMO.

Pictures and videos are often carefully curated to highlight how well the life of a person is going or how much fun they are having. This can then create a feeling that others are achieving more or having more fun. This FOMO can lead to anxiety, depression, and increase the urge to engage in activities you might not normally be inclined to.

While there is a lot on social media that is true, or a part of people's lives, it is important to remember that what people put out isn't all that is happening in their lives. People often post more about the highlights than about their struggles. So, if you compare your life to what a person chooses to show the world, you will be comparing yourself to someone whose life you don't fully know.

I think it is important to mention that it is unhealthy to assume that even when people are showing highlights of their lives, they are exaggerating or being untrue. Your satisfaction with your life shouldn't be based on your assumption that others are not having it as great as they seem to be. Your satisfaction with your life should come internally and should not be hinged on others. This is a much healthier way to live life.

Social media's trend culture is also something you might feel FOMO towards. Whether it's a dance trend on TikTok or a fashion trend on Instagram, trends tend to gain traction fast and can make you feel like you should participate because everyone else is doing it. I am intentional about not jumping on trends because things in trend often go out of trend. And if the trend is something I feel—even if just a little bit—that I will regret having joined in, I don't participate.

2. Career and life achievements:

It is possible to feel FOMO because of the career paths people you know seem to be taking or the achievements they seem to have. You might feel the pressure to choose a certain course in school, maybe Medicine, Computer Science, or Music, because your friends are also doing so, and you don't want to be left out.

I do believe that people in our lives can positively influence our career choices, but there is a thin line between you choosing a career path you genuinely enjoy and choosing one because you want to have what other people have.

When you begin to make decisions about what course to study and where you might want to work, it is important to consider your interests, your strengths, the things that intrigue you, that excite you. Remember that if you go down a path simply because someone else is doing it, you might be setting yourself up to struggle on a path that isn't even yours.

Apart from career choices, you might face FOMO regarding attending every career event, workshop, or conference you hear about. Again, your friends can be instrumental in helping you find important events and even encourage you to attend them when you do not have the drive or willingness. However, this can also lead to FOMO when you know that the event or workshop might not be the best use of your time, and you could be engaging in other meaningful activities.

3. Social activities:

I spoke about attending parties earlier in this chapter, and that is one of the many social activities you might feel FOMO towards. These activities might be fun for some people, but for those who do not want to participate, the fear of not fitting in or being the odd one in the group can lead to anxiety and FOMO.

Other social activities include going to a friend's event, attending a concert with a group of friends, going to a particular game night, etc. While these things are not bad in and of themselves, participating in them simply because of FOMO can make you vulnerable to doing whatever it takes to identify with the group, and might lead to decisions that might have devastating consequences.

4. Romantic relationships and sex:

In the previous chapter, I spoke about how mainstream media makes romantic relationships something to aspire to because it is cool to have and speak about. This can often cause pressure to be in a relationship, whether you think it's healthy or not, and can make you experience lots of FOMO when it seems like people are in relationships everywhere you turn. In this digital age, it is even easier to keep track of who is in a relationship, with whom, since when, what they do, where they go, and so on. This can create an intense amount of FOMO, as you may feel like you are missing out on an important experience.

Closely tied with the FOMO of romantic relationships is the FOMO concerning having sex or engaging in sexual activities. Like many other things, your background, your values and convictions, your social circle, the conversation around this subject that you've been exposed to, and your sense of self, will influence the intensity of FOMO you feel concerning sex.

If you are in a circle where *coolness* is defined by how sexually active a person is, then you might feel a lot more pressure than someone whose circle has completely different views on sex.

A note on purity:

As a teenager, my mum and I would have conversations about purity. She would remind me that God honors those who choose to keep themselves. We live in a world that makes purity feel old school, like it's a form of bondage. But it's still God's will today, like it was a thousand years ago.

Remember that at the end of the day, you are the one who holds the power to make your own decisions.

5. Hard drugs and alcohol:

This is another area where you might feel FOMO in and out of school. This is because there might be a belief that those who engage in taking hard drugs and can stand the effects of alcohol are the *cool kids.* If this is a perception you have, I want to let you know that this is untrue. Taking these things doesn't make you any cooler, and if anything, they harm your body. Multiple studies have shown the harmful effects of taking hard drugs and drinking alcohol on your physical and mental health. I know it might seem like a fun thing to try out, but know that engaging in activities that harm your body is never beneficial.

There are many more areas you might feel FOMO depending on where you are in life and who you are surrounded with. One thing to always remember is that you don't have to do something just because everyone is doing it.

Tips on handling FOMO:

1. Surround yourself with the right people:

Most times, the people who surround us influence us. If you notice that your circle of friends is constantly asking you to do things that go against your values, it is an indication that the circle is not the best for you. Try to connect with people, whether in-person or online, who help bring out the best in you, rather than make you who you are not or do not want to be. These people will also help look out for you when you are in situations that draw you to engage in activities that might not be the best for you.

2. Understand what fun means to you:

I realized that having my own definition of fun early on in college helped me be content with not doing what others were doing. To me, fun looked like hanging out in my room and chatting with my friends; it meant watching a movie with friends; it meant cooking and singing in a friend's apartment; it meant going bowling with some people in JAMS. You get the gist.

It's also okay if what you consider fun is not what others enjoy (so far, it's not harming you or anybody). Knowing what counts as fun to you can greatly help you in handling FOMO.

3. Focus on nurturing yourself:

Instead of comparing your life to that of your friends, friends of friends, celebrities, and every other person online, focus on nurturing yourself. This will help you channel the energy of comparison into building depth in the things you love and/or are interested in, and will help you feel more content and fulfilled.

As Ikanna Okim would say, if you have time to be hung up on

what other people are doing and achieving, then you are not spending enough time on yourself.

4. Limit your use of social media:

As I mentioned earlier, social media is one of the main sources of FOMO. A good practice is to limit the amount of time you spend on these apps to ensure that you are not spending an unhealthy amount of time online.

When I arrived at Bowdoin in 2021, I turned off all my Instagram notifications and removed it from my home screen. I wanted to remove it from my view as much as possible without deleting the app. These actions helped me curtail my social media use so much that I began to use the app less, just by doing those alone. About a year later, I did the same thing for WhatsApp. My goal was to be able to check the notifications and messages I get on these apps in my own time, rather than just whenever a notification came in.

I also think social media is hyper-stimulating, so I enjoyed not getting notifications from either of these platforms. I cannot begin to explain how mindful it has made me of my social media use. I encourage you to try the same thing—to make a conscious effort to take charge of your social media, rather than let it take charge of you. You will be happy you did it.

5. Seek help:

Seeking help is always a good idea when you are struggling with anything, FOMO included. You can speak to your friends, family members, teachers, mentors, professionals, or anyone you know who can provide guidance and can be a listening ear to you. Please don't try to navigate this alone. Reach out if you need help. You'll be surprised to see how eager people are to help when you reach out honestly.

Your journey is different.

There is a quote from one of the thought leaders, John Obidi, whom I have learned from over the years: "Your fight is different."

My first encounter with this phrase was on Facebook in 2017, and it has stayed with me since then. This phrase is one of the reminders I held on throughout my time at Bowdoin as I have navigated being in a place with so much privilege. I was constantly reminding myself that I did not have the same luxuries, whether that be being a U.S. citizen, coming from a wealthy home, many of my classmates had. This is not to diminish those things that they have. No, I love it for them. But I had to be honest with myself about what I had and what that meant for me.

This meant that if people were inviting me to a movie night and I knew I had an important assignment due, I had to prioritize that. I could always go to the movie night another weekend, but those grades would stay with me.

In my sophomore year, one of my very good friends, Dulra, sent me a message saying:

> ***"Your struggles are different. You didn't choose your battles when you were born. They were chosen for you. But now, you have the option to either fight the battle with superior positioning or you can succumb to FOMO and forget that you're built differently."***

It's been years since he sent it to me, but it still feels so relevant. I knew what I was dreaming of, and I had to constantly decide to not simply do what everyone else was doing but instead make sure it would not negatively impact my own journey.

The reality is that you're the one who knows your journey best. You know how far you've come and where you want to go. If you do what every other person is doing just because you want to belong, the price you'll pay and the consequences you might have to live with may be heavy. Make choices you know the future you will be proud of. I'm cheering you on.

Please make your notes here:

CHAPTER 15

Managing your finances

"Don't tell me where your priorities are. Show me where you spend your money, and I'll tell you what they are

— James W. Frick

Money! Money! Money! Let's talk about money.

I have always been a frugal spender, and if you ask me why, I might say it's partially because of how and where I grew up. Since I grew up in a low-income family, spending frugally was the norm. My parents had to spend strategically to take care of my family, and, unconsciously, that was the model of spending I first saw. Then, I lived with the Nwozors, and they exposed me to a different type of financial lifestyle. Although the Nwozors didn't have to be as frugal in their spending as my parents were, they were still moderate spenders, and that continued to foster my frugal lifestyle.

I acknowledge that people might be at very different places financially and hope that you can still take away important lessons from this chapter, regardless of where you are.

Tips on maintaining your finances as a student:

- ***Spend intentionally:***
  Impulse spending is real and is an issue that can often go

unnoticed for a long time. Sometimes it might only show up during holiday periods where stores are having discounts, when you go shopping, or when you're with friends. I often remind myself not to buy things if I don't need them, even when they are at discounted prices. Although these sales can go a long way at certain times, they can also make us spend more than we need to, or when we don't even need to spend at all.

- ***Track your spending:***

Coming to Bowdoin meant a change in my spending habits. As a first-year student, I had to learn the best times to get my necessities, how to look up good deals, and more, in this new environment. I honestly did not start tracking my spending until my junior year because I didn't think I needed to, since I was not someone who spent much and had a pretty good discipline when it comes to spending. However, when I started tracking my spending, I realized how much more intentional I became about what I was spending on.

Tracking your spending helps you understand where your finances are going and makes you reflect on what is taking the most of your money.

- ***Start and/or continue saving:***

A few days after I finished reading my first personal finance book, I went on a walk with my brother, Stephen, and I told him that the book made me realize that just because I was not a big spender didn't automatically make me a big saver. To my credit, I had been saving money I received as gifts in the three years of my senior secondary school days, but I didn't continue actively saving when I arrived at college.

Saving is a good way to set aside money for your future. You don't have to have a particular goal to save, and this is something I had to remind myself. The money you save can help you in diverse ways—from personal expenses to emergencies, helping someone in need, and more. I know that saving can be difficult based on your situation. I completely understand. I hope that if you are in a situation where you can save, even if just a tiny bit, you make it a habit. Trust me, you will be glad you did.

- ***Create a budget:***

Budgeting is the flip side of tracking your spending. Here, you allocate how much you want to spend on different categories of things.

I didn't start budgeting until junior year, and while I was already doing a good job without it, it helped increase my intentionality with how I was sending my money. Creating a budget helped me monitor when I was overspending and helped me track expenses I hadn't planned for. It also helped me reallocate my money when necessary. For instance, when I spent less than I anticipated in a given month, I could move the extra to my savings, use the rollover funds for my expenses the next month, or get myself something.

Budgeting is a good way to stay in charge of your finances rather than letting things happen on their own.

- ***Invest in yourself:***

Money can be a great tool to get where you need to be, whether it's to school, attain a new mastery, or even to take care of yourself. Investing in yourself is the best investment you can make and an act that will give back to you in more ways than you can imagine.

If there is a course you want to take or a training that will bring you closer to where you want to be, spending your money to acquire that skill or knowledge will benefit you tremendously.

- ***Carve your own financial plan:***

As a student, it might feel challenging to find financial plans that are tailored to your needs and circumstances. I faced this myself. Before coming to college, I heard of the 50-30-20 rule, which says you should use 50% of your income for your needs, 30% for your wants, and 20% for savings. However, this did not apply to me because I did not need to spend up to 50% of my income from my on-campus job on my needs. I also paid my monthly 10% tithe, which the formula did not seem to account for.

So, I decided to save between 30% to 50% of my income, depending on my expenses that month, ensure I always paid my tithe of 10%, used around 10% of my income for my wants, and used the rest of my income, between 30% to 50%, for my needs.

I share this to show you that you don't have to be rigid with your financial plan. I encourage you to look up resources that fit your needs, but if you don't find any, you can always adapt what you find.

The key thing is to ensure you are allocating a good amount of your money, whether from your income, pocket money, gifts, or other sources, to the important categories like saving, needs, and wants.

- ***The act of giving***.

"We make a living by what we get, but we make a life by what we give," said Winston Churchill.

In February 2025, I was at an annual conference for Christian students across the country called Veritas Weekend. After a session with two people in academia who had come to faith later in their lives, I thanked the facilitator for his wonderful facilitation. As we spoke, he said something that struck me. He said, "It is important to show people that they don't have to be just takers, they can be givers too."

The moment I heard this statement, I wanted to shout "Yes!" In just a few words, he had captured one of the core life lessons I had learned in these past few years. As someone who has been a beneficiary of a lot of the generosity of institutions and various people, I have learned that I don't have to just be a recipient; I can, and should, also pay it forward. You can too!

As a Christian, the Bible shapes my worldview, and a Scripture that beautifully captures this is "It is more blessed to give than to receive," from Acts 20:35. At first, that verse might seem counterintuitive because ordinarily, when you give, you're parting with what you have. In this sense, giving should cause you to have less. But giving actually brings more. As a result, the giver can continue to give. This is why they say givers never lack, and I've experienced this time and time again.

The first time I thought, "I'm surely going to give back to Bowdoin financially," was after my first year at Bowdoin. I had studied in Germany over the summer, and when I got back, I felt a new kind of gratitude towards whoever the donors for my grant were. The realization that someone set up a grant years ago for students they didn't know and might never meet to help those students pursue their interests was a beautiful thing to experience. I was learning to call the world home because of someone else's generosity, and this inspired me. I wanted to be able to do the same thing.

I've given to family, friends, and more during my time at Bowdoin, but this is something I rarely speak about. I give because I believe my finances are not meant to simply meet my needs, but to also meet the needs of those around me as well. While giving is a constant in my life, I rarely speak about it because I never want to get to a place where I start to feel too important because of how much I give or the ways my finances are supporting people. I know there is nothing I have that I haven't been given, and I always want to see giving as a privilege.

- ***Paying tithes and offerings.***

In September 2023, I gave the largest tithe I had ever given, and I had mixed feelings. Honestly, as I went to the website, I kept questioning myself and considering whether to do it. I had actually been thinking about it for several weeks. "Do I really have to?" I asked myself. "Wasn't it a grant I received?" As I was asking myself these questions, I became even more convinced that since the grant was income for my work over the summer, I should pay my tithe.

More than that, paying my tithe was a gesture that would reemphasize God's place in my work and career path, and by extension, in my life. As I wrestled with whether or not to give my tithe, I reflected on how humbling it was, really, to be able to give that much to God. It reminded me of how I used to save in secondary school and make efforts to pay my offerings whenever I got money. And you know what my mum told me when I visited home? She told me she saw the slip where I wrote my pledge to a church project, and she was struck by my faithfulness. I was so emotional hearing that.

Throughout my time at Bowdoin, I've stayed consistent with paying my tithes, because it has been my way of acknowledging that there is nothing I have that God hasn't given me. Giving that tithe in September 2023 reminded me of the Scripture that says, "He that is faithful in very little will also be faithful in much." Looking back, I feel teary to see what God has done, how he keeps rewarding me, and I'm so thankful that he has blessed me with *much.*

- ***Financial literacy is key.***

I read my first personal finance book in the summer of 2023, the summer when I interned at the Lagos University Teaching Hospital (LUTH).

I had spoken with Daniel about wanting to rebuild my reading habits, and one day, while on Instagram, I decided to check John Obidi's highlights for his book recommendations. I saw many good books, but one that stood out to me was *The Richest Man in Babylon* because I had heard of it several times.

I asked Daniel about it, and he gave it a 9/10 rating, which was encouraging. After speaking about it for a bit, he sent me the soft copy, and two days later, I began to read it. Seven days later, I had completed the book, and I sent Daniel a text saying, "I have successfully come to the end of what was a beautiful reading journey! From the age-old wisdom about making and keeping money, to the very profound lessons about lending, borrowing, and paying off debts, I can't help but look at money differently now."

I enjoyed reading the book because it reminded me of things I had learned growing up, while also offering new insights. I had always known that savings are crucial for our finances, but seeing it in the form of a story and imagining the ways it related to me was instrumental in helping me take action. *The Richest Man in Babylon* was so insightful for me that I began to wonder what other financial knowledge I was missing because I wasn't reading books. This was the beginning of my journey to increasing my financial literacy.

A few weeks after I returned to Bowdoin for my third year, my brother sent me an episode from the podcast called *Diary of a CEO,* and that episode was called *The Money Expert: Do Not Buy A House,* which Stephen Bartley recorded with Morgan Housel. In that episode, Morgan Housel shared nuggets from his book, *The Psychology of Money,* and it reminded me of how much wisdom I could get from books.

That December, I decided to go to Germany for another study abroad program, and the day I got to my host sister's place, I saw a copy of Housel's book on her bed. Imagine my shock the moment I stepped into her room and saw the book I had been longing to read for a few weeks. About a week later, I was on a call with a friend, and this same book came up. I was convinced that it was my final sign to get my copy of the book. So early in January 2024, I purchased my copy of *The Psychology of Money.* I took the book with me to school every day and read it on the train, in restaurants as I waited for my food, and when I was back at the apartment. I was reading it so much that by the third week of January, when I left Germany, I had finished the whole book.

In the summer that followed, I was digging through my huge stack of books and found a personal finance book I had purchased the summer before: *The Smart Money Woman* by Arese Ugwu, and I decided it was time for me to finally read it. I started taking the book with me when I went to my Neuroscience Lab every day and read it while waiting for a part of my experiment to run, and during my lunch breaks. In a few weeks, I had read the whole book and had officially finished reading my third personal finance book.

In my senior year, I read my fourth personal finance book called *Mind Your Money* by Yanely Espinal. Since I had started saving and budgeting at this point, I was able to take additional steps regarding my spending and saving as I read the book. The book also added more knowledge about things that the other books hadn't extensively spoken about—the complexities of using a credit card, loans, investments, and more.

You might be wondering why I was reading these many personal finance books, and the answer is simple: I wanted to be as knowledgeable as I can about my finances. I knew I had to be committed to my financial literacy if I was going to be able to make informed and wise decisions for the present and future me.

If you are also hoping to build a healthier financial life and are looking for books to start with, the four books I mentioned are good places to start. Yanely Espinal's book also has more resources on practical personal finance tips for students that I know you will find helpful.

Your money mindset matters.

Understanding your money mindset is an important part of your personal finance journey. Your background, social media, your friends, etc., might have influenced your money mindset. Your money mindset might be the reason you spend the way you do, why you find it easy or hard to save, and why you have the relationship you have with money.

Before you use any of the tips I outlined above, I encourage you to reflect on your relationship with money. Feel free to use the blank after this chapter as a place to start.

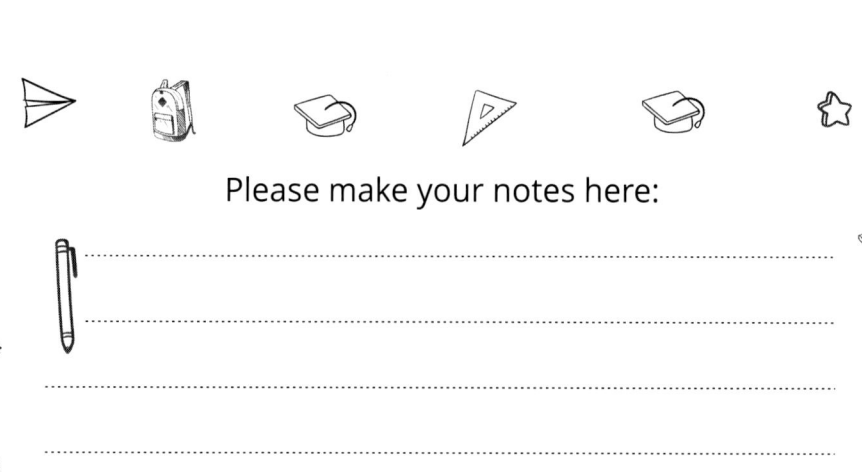

Please make your notes here:

CHAPTER 16

Shining your light and leaving a legacy

"Let your light so shine before men, that they may see your good works, and glorify your Father which is in heaven."

—Matthew 5:16 (KJV)

On my nineteenth birthday, I had one of the most beautiful celebrations I have ever had.

A few weeks prior, Cath had asked me which of my friends I would invite to my wedding. I thought that was an interesting question for her to ask in our second year in college, and I thought it was just a question about friendships, so I answered. Little did I know that she was using my answer to compile a list of people to invite to my birthday celebration.

So, when the night of my birthday came and she asked me if I had anything planned, I didn't think much of her question. But when we began to make plans for us to go on a walk, I began to suspect she was on to something. To my great surprise, Cath had brought together a room of twenty-one of my friends on a Tuesday night, in the season of midterm exams, to celebrate with me.

For those who were at my birthday and even those who couldn't make it, she crafted a book with birthday wishes and pictures of me with different people in my communities. Not only did she do that, she reached out to several alumni and another friend who was studying abroad at the time to send in videos, which she turned into a video compilation.

This birthday celebration made me incredibly emotional. Earlier that day, I had cried three different times because of the clash of emotions I felt about having an exam on my birthday and the expectation to feel happy and celebrate. So ending the day surrounded by friends and with the most heartwarming notes and clips was more than I could ask for.

As I watched the videos and read the notes, a common thing my friends said was how I was such a light on campus. *Light!*

This is something I didn't come to Bowdoin expecting I would be called, but it made so much sense that people would call me that—I was simply reflecting God's light.

I felt incredibly humbled to know that my presence lit up rooms and helped other people see their paths more clearly. As I returned to my room that night, I wrote in my journal, "I pray I never lose that shine, spark, love, warmth, resilience, and positive impact that people could not stop mentioning."

That birthday was a timely reminder that I had been called to be a light wherever I was sent. Shining the light God has put in me wasn't a choice; it was part of my very being.

Knowing that shining my light was a state of being was crucial to remember, because in my junior year, I had many moments where I was overly concerned about making all the right moves and doing all the perfect things to shine my light. I had to remind myself that I didn't need to try to be perfect to shine my light; I simply had to allow God to move through me.

Shine!

Several Scriptures have defined my time at Bowdoin, and one of them is "Let your light so shine before men that they may see your good works and glorify your father in heaven" (Matthew 5:16). I always loved this Scripture growing up. And when I got to Bowdoin, it was a Scripture I would quote to myself as I navigated the space I took up and the ways I showed up.

I want you to shine your light—unapologetically. I know that people might not like how you take up space, the way you compose yourself, the things you choose to be a part of or refrain from, but I want you to keep shining. There is no virtue in dimming your light because you are worried about what people will say about you.

As a Christian, I know I am called to be a reflection of God's light wherever I am, and I live by that calling. I know that I would be doing myself and the rest of the world a great disservice if I did not use the talent, intellect, and resources God has given me to make the world a better place. I'm flipping this over to you. You cannot be hidden. You should not be.

In April 2025, I was sharing some of my key lessons with a high school student when she said, "I want to go to a small school so people can know me." I smiled at her before reminding her that she didn't need to go to a small school to feel seen. She could be seen in a large or small school. The size of her school didn't have to determine how far and brightly her light shone. She could shine in a large school as much as she could in a small school.

When I think of shining my light, I think of taking up space. There is so much you can be and do when you enter the right spaces. I want you to enter places and make them better than you met them. Let the value you carry seep into every place you go, so much that when you leave, your impact lives on.

Making an impact.

Do you know we're all capable of making an impact? Yes, you, reading this, can create a tangible and long-lasting impact in the world.

I know it can sometimes feel like only people who have attained a certain educational or work level can create positive change, but you also can in your corner. You don't have to do something international for it to be considered an impact. Even if you are only able to reach one person, even if you are the reason two students now know that despite their background, they, too, can pursue a career in pharmacy, law, or music, you have made an impact.

Leaving a legacy.

"Ruth, you've shown us that it can be done," is a remark a student made the evening after I was awarded two of Bowdoin's highest honors for students—the President's Award and the Dunlap Prize.

Every year, the President's award is presented to one or two students from the graduating class who have demonstrated leadership and outstanding contributions to life at Bowdoin, as well as outstanding personal achievements, and it was a huge honor to have been selected as the 2025 recipient of that award.

The General R. H. Dunlap prize is also awarded to one or two graduating students who compose the best essay about service and have demonstrated "exceptional service for the benefit of society."

I was honored to receive these awards in recognition of my leadership and service at Bowdoin, and I was thankful to be signing off my time at Bowdoin with such a legacy. I have learned not to get involved in all the activities just for the accolades, because they are nowhere as fulfilling as knowing that you had a real impact. This is something that has guided me in my leadership and service at Bowdoin. In fact, I did not know of the Dunlap Prize until about two months before my graduation. Awards have never been a motivation.

Beyond the awards, I was satisfied to know that I had inspired students I had interacted with, mentored, or advised at one point or the other to strive to be the best they can be while at Bowdoin. I was intentional about being a grounding presence for others, contributing to all the spaces I entered in the best way I could, looking after those around me, and living out my Christian faith. Without realizing it, I was building a legacy that would stay long after I left Bowdoin.

In April of my final semester, I received many heartwarming messages as I started signing out of my leadership roles. I was moved by all those messages, and they reminded me of how important it is for leaders to feel loved and appreciated. One note, from Andy, said:

> ***"To Ruth: You've done such a great job at not only leading Africa Alliance but also showing us that a leader can lead with love. You're such a rock for many students in this community. YOU DA BEST!"***

What an honor to have had such an impact.

At the beginning of this book, I mentioned that I struggled with writing this book because I didn't think I had enough to share. For months, I was asking myself if I had enough to say, if I had enough to give. Yet, I knew I could not let my doubts and fears stop me from leaving a worthy legacy. So, I wrote. This book is not in your hands because I did not have any fears; it's in your hands because I wrote despite having a lot of fears.

How do you want to be remembered when you leave a space, when you leave your school, when you leave that club you're a part of? What do you want your legacy to be? Would people be able to say that you left a place better than you found it?

One of my biggest desires is that you thrive, wherever you are, not just survive. Wherever you are, whether in high school, college, or a later stage of your life, I hope you will make a mark and leave a legacy.

Where does your worth lie?

I can't encourage you to shine your light, to thrive, without speaking about the subject of worth.

Before you read on, I want you to do something for me. Take a few seconds to think about where you place your worth. Is it in the things you do, the things you have achieved, the people you're surrounded by, or something else? This question is crucial because if you don't know where your worth lies, where it *should lie,* you will let the wrong things define you.

In February 2025, I was on a panel at a conference—Veritas Weekend. I had attended for 4 years in a row, and on the panel for the second morning, one of the panelists, a Christian psychiatrist, said, "We have to remind people that their worth does not just lie in what they do; they are much more than that."

This struck me because it is true. I have heard repeatedly to not put my worth in what I do, but in the *Person* who made me.

Knowing that my output does not define my worth gives me a more balanced approach to life, one where I am striving to shine my light daily and be the best I can be while knowing that my worth is not attached to whatever I achieve. So I ask again, where does your worth lie?

Please make your notes here:

CHAPTER 17

Preparing for life after college

"The best preparation for tomorrow is doing your best today."

—H. Jackson Brown, Jr.

When I started my journey at Bowdoin, I wasn't thinking of how it would come to an end someday. But as the end of my junior year drew closer, I began to reflect on the limited amount of time I had to spend in college. One day, I would no longer be able to walk from my class to my favorite study spot in Hatch Library. I wouldn't be able to head to the dining halls to grab dinner with a friend, or host events with my clubs on campus, and hang out in the common room with first-year students living in my dorm. One day, my college experience would end.

College is a temporary place, and this realization is important for how you view your time there. This very understanding of the temporary nature of our college experiences was one of the motivations for this book, Dear Sojourner. Your time in college is a sojourn, a defining journey. Nobody comes to college to stay in college. Although our reasons for coming might be different, our time in college will end at one point or the other.

When in college, many of your experiences might be curated for you. Events are organized by your school or clubs and societies on campus, you see your friends regularly because of classes or other events, and you might be around your friends in a way you never might be again. This is why the transition out of college might be jarring when you're no longer in that *bubble.*

Knowing the transient nature of our college experiences and the change that comes with transitioning out of college, I need to spend some time speaking about how you can prepare for life after college.

At the time of my writing this, I haven't graduated from Bowdoin, so the lessons I share here are things I am reflecting on in real time. Most of the lessons I will share have already been mentioned in different chapters. This chapter offers a chance for me to bring those points together to help you see how they connect with your future and how you can start or continue planning for life after college. The tips I will share are only a fraction of the things you can do to prepare for post-college life, but this is a good place to start.

How to prepare for post-college life:

1. Utilize the opportunities around you:

In the chapter on opportunities, I spoke about the different ways opportunities present themselves to us and how you can make the best use of them. These opportunities, whether big or small, can help prepare you for life after college. Many times, graduate schools, employers, or other people want to see how you utilized the opportunities you had so they can help you access new ones. These opportunities might also give you the experience and skills needed to thrive in the spaces you aspire to enter.

2. Build or strengthen your network:

Regardless of whether you already have a vast network or you're building one, you can always strengthen your network. Doing so while in college will help prepare you for life after. Your network will be crucial in your post-college life, impacting your job opportunities, the spaces you are a part of, and how you view the world.

3. Be intentional about financial literacy:

Leaving college without adequate financial literacy can be more harmful than you realize. It's important to know how to spend your money properly, how to budget, save, invest, and more. Adulthood requires that you be in charge of your finances, and you will not be able to do that unless you take the time to learn more about finances.

4. Develop important soft skills:

To thrive after college, you need to develop certain soft skills. These include communication, teamwork, time management, problem solving, conflict management, public speaking, and more. These skills are vital for your relationships, workplace, and how you interact with people overall.

5. Prepare your professional documents:

As you prepare for life after college, it is important to get the professional documents that are often required when applying to jobs, graduate schools, fellowships, or simply connecting with people. You will need a professional-looking headshot, whether it is with a regular camera or a phone. Also, open a LinkedIn profile if you don't have one. LinkedIn is a great place to expand your network and document your work. You also need to have a resume so that when opportunities come your way, you are ready to seize them.

6. Know that there is no one perfect path to take:

In my Sophomore year at Bowdoin, I attended Bowdoin's Annual Sophomore Bootcamp. Sophomore Bootcamp is a three-day-long series of career workshops organized by Bowdoin's career office for sophomores before the beginning of the spring semester.

During one of the sessions in the Bootcamp, we did what we

called the *values and skills* exercises. Here, we started by brainstorming the values that were the most important for us in our workplaces. Then, we wrote out the skills we had and the jobs that fit those skills, plus the work values that were important for us.

By the end of the session, I realized that there were more places I could thrive in than I had thought, and there were multiple paths I could take to achieve my dreams of building equitable healthcare systems. Although becoming a physician is what I was most passionate about, it was not the only career path I could take to contribute to medicine and have a fulfilling life.

The thought of taking the *perfect path* can be overwhelming and end up stopping us from taking any steps at all. This is why it is important to remember that you don't have to do things perfectly to succeed. You also will most likely not have a linear path, and that is normal. Life is full of twists and turns that all contribute to what we learn and who we eventually become.

Where to next?

At the end of your college career, you will transition to a different chapter of your life. Some people have always known what that chapter will be, whether it is graduate school or a job, but others might not. Regardless of what category you fall under, reflecting on the question of "Where do I want to go after this?" is a worthwhile thing to do.

If you feel unsure of where that is or what you want to do in the future, you're not alone. Before coming to college, I thought that everyone in college knew exactly what they wanted to do in the future and the paths they would take. The college essays I had to write for my applications often had questions about what I hoped to do in the future, so I thought that meant once you got into college, your path would be clear and you'd be set. This was far from reality.

In college, I met people who came in thinking they wanted to pursue medicine but realized their interest in medicine wasn't truly theirs, but one they had taken on because of family, friends, and other external influences. I've also interacted with people from different schools who, in their final year of college, are unsure of what career they want to pursue right after college or long term.

The key thing is to be willing to learn more about yourself and your interests as you grow, knowing that your interests can change, and understanding that you don't have to have your whole future figured out to take the first step. You might also need to try out more than one role before you figure out what career path you want to pursue long term.

Please make your notes here:

CHAPTER 18

My faith, my anchor

"Faith is not believing in my own unshakable belief. Faith is believing an unshakable God when everything in me trembles and quakes."

—Beth Moore

One night in my senior year, I hosted two students recently accepted into Bowdoin as part of the program for an event called *Bearings in Brunswick.* This event is where Bowdoin invites admitted students to visit campus and explore the student experience over a few days. That night, as they sat on my wine-colored couch, they asked me about different parts of my college experience. As we spoke, I learned that they were both Christians, which was heartwarming to hear.

I leaned against a wall in my room and began to share how my faith has grown at Bowdoin. "At Bowdoin," I told them, "I got to intentionally choose to be a Christian. I wasn't just doing it because I was born into a Christian family; I was doing it because I had made the decision."

Before I arrived at Bowdoin, I was eager to find a Christian community because my faith has always been a big part of my life. I remember searching the list of clubs so I could find Christian clubs on campus. I wanted to be sure I would find a community to be a part of.

Over the years, I have grown in my faith in ways I didn't while at home. I have asked questions I didn't while growing up, wrestled with answers I didn't understand, and had conversations with people with different beliefs. All these things contributed to my growth and helped me develop an even deeper understanding of my Christian walk and a deeper relationship with God.

My journey to the U.S. is a testament that God does know the end from the beginning and is capable of doing more than we ask or think, more than our wildest dreams. When I left for the U.S., my mum would occasionally remind me of why she gave me my Igbo name and how it is a reflection of how God has directed my path from my birth until now.

If you ask me the biggest reason I wrote this book, I will tell you it's because I felt led to do so. Led by whom? By God. This book was one of His legacy mandates for me at Bowdoin.

But my journey with my faith hasn't been smooth. I have had many low moments, several of which I am still processing.

I will share two themes with you.

Dealing with anxiety.

The first time I could tell I was having an anxiety attack was one evening in the spring semester of my junior year. I had just gotten back from a meeting, and I sat down in Druck, one of the science academic buildings. I had a lot I needed to work on and had been thinking of them all day, so as I settled down, I began to feel my chest tighten. Shortly after, I started to heave. I was finding it difficult to breathe.

I didn't know what was happening or what to do, so I texted one of my friends, Afia, all I was feeling, and after describing it to her, she pointed out that I might be having an anxiety attack. At first, I did not think that was what was happening, but as I paid more attention to how I was feeling and read extensively about what an anxiety attack was, I realized that was what it was. For the first time, I was putting a name to this feeling I had felt a few times in my freshman and junior years, but had not paid more attention to.

I felt a lot of anxiety in my freshman year of college, so much so that when I wrote my piece for the annual JAMS magazine, my topic was on anxiety from the lens of a character in the Bible we had read a little about.

The newness of many things in my first year of college and my distance from home and family contributed to the anxiety I felt. I also had very high expectations for myself, so anytime I felt like I was not meeting those expectations, I got anxious. Very anxious.

I remember sitting at my desk in my freshman dorm one afternoon, feeling my chest tighten more and more as the seconds passed. I didn't know what was happening, I didn't know what to do, so I just sat there, almost in tears, trying to breathe as well as I could.

In my freshman year, I became intentional about giving God all my worries and telling Him about my fears. I kept relearning that I was not doing life on my own, and I have a guide who is constantly interceding for me. I was learning that I did not need to do everything or be overly busy, but let God lead me concerning where to go and what to be involved with.

In my junior year, the anxiety attacks returned more frequently. I had gone through sophomore year with little to no attacks, so having them resurface in junior year was not a good sign. This called for a renewed reflection on the things on my mind and where I was putting my trust. I did not have to let anxiety get the best of me. In fact, it shouldn't.

Anxiety is something many people deal with in different seasons of life. My faith in God and His Word greatly helped me not to be drowned by the overwhelming feeling of anxiety. When I didn't know where to go or what to do, I could always lean on God. This is an assurance I'll hold onto as I go through life.

Dealing with Uncertainty.

There's a sticker on my iPad that says "I don't know what tomorrow holds, but I know who holds tomorrow," and it has served as a powerful reminder for me over the years.

On April 30, 2025, I received a rejection email from one of the forty jobs I applied to, starting in December 2024. Although I didn't get a rejection from all forty (for some, I never even heard back; for others, I had one, two, and even four interviews), I didn't get the jobs. Every rejection was heartbreaking, but I was learning not to let the rejections ruin the rest of my day.

A few weeks before I received that email, I was sitting at my desk at one of my on-campus jobs, journaling instead of completing my tasks. I couldn't face those tasks because even though I had been trying so hard not to feel stressed about the whole job search process, I found myself feeling teary at different (and often unexpected) times. That was exactly how I was feeling that April morning at work.

In March and April of my senior year, every time I spent time thinking about how stressful that season had been, my throat would tighten and tears would well up in my eyes.

You know how people say, "If someone had told me… I would have laughed."? I always found that to be an interesting statement to make because I didn't fully believe they would have laughed or dismissed what the person said, like they were claiming.

But this was actually my case.

If you had told me on December 10, 2024, the day I applied to my first position, that by the end of April 2025, I would still be applying to jobs, I really would have laughed. In my mind, the latest I would still be applying for jobs would be February 2025. But two months beyond February, I was still applying.

I was worried that if I was still applying later than February, I wouldn't be able to get my work authorization in time. Ironically, I received my job authorization in March, months earlier than I had expected. I had my work authorization approved, but did not have a job.

How incredible! We truly can't predict the future.

I have had different seasons in my college career where I dealt with uncertainty, but none of this magnitude.

I had dealt with uncertainty whether my plan to intern in Nigeria after my sophomore year would work out, or if I would find housing when I studied abroad in Germany the second time. Despite all the uncertainty, I saw God come through for me in marvelous ways. From helping me get an approval for my job the day my application for a grant was due to providing housing for me in Munich with the best Nigerian host sister I could have hoped for, He showed me that even when I couldn't see any way, *He* had a way.

My final semester stretched my faith to a great extent. I was reminded that trusting God is not something I do only when things are going in a way I understand. Trust is a state of mind to maintain despite not understanding what God is doing.

I see God's promises in the Bible, I hear it in songs, I know it—deep down I do—because God has come through for me time and time again. Yet, in the face of uncertainty, I shudder and worry, because it is only human to do so.

So, I continue to constantly remind myself that God will work things out. I know it, I've seen it, I've lived it. My life is a testimony of what God can do. So why would he fail now?

Dreams bigger than me.

Writing this whole book is a dream so much bigger than me that it took me months to accept and start writing. How could I possibly write to students here in the U.S., back home in Nigeria, and around the world?

In February 2025, when I began laying out the logistics for publishing this book, I was struck by the amount of money that would need to go into it. I remember texting two of my brothers and two close friends and telling them my concerns about the cost.

I was planning to give out as many copies as I could in the U.S. and Nigeria after the launch, and that meant I would have to print out several copies of my book for my first launch.

For weeks, I was restless about the enormous task of writing and financing a book on my own. I didn't feel like I could handle what I had to do, nor could I fund it. I was becoming too worried about the logistics, which was impacting how I was approaching writing the book.

Then one day, Bukola, one of my first editors, sent me a beautiful and important reminder that this book is God's work and He would fund it. She reminded me that "more often than not, God gives us assignments that seem bigger than our current capacity." She emphasized that "our stepping out in faith, even when we don't see the resources yet, is His [God's] expected response from us."

This was such a timely reminder for me because God had been trying to tell me that this book project wasn't about my capacity, but the mandate He had given me. I felt like this project was a lot bigger than I could handle, that it was much bigger than me, but *that* was the point.

Although I have shared a lot about my story in this book, it's more than me. It's about how God has worked *in me* throughout these past four years and how the lessons from my time in college can serve others in various stages of their lives.

Living in answered prayers.

My time at Bowdoin always reminded me that I was living in answered prayers. For years, I had prayed about studying abroad, and here I was doing more than I had known was possible. This understanding is something that constantly keeps me grateful and serves as a reminder of God's faithfulness when I become too worried about the future and whether it will work out.

I don't need anyone to show me proof that God answers prayers. I'm living proof.

Please make your notes here:

CHAPTER 19

Staying grateful

"The more you practice the art of thankfulness, the more you have to be thankful for."

—Norman Vincent Peale

Gosh! I don't know where to even start on the subject of gratitude.

Practicing gratitude is a key thing that has helped me avoid taking the opportunities I have for granted. It has helped me stay grounded even when things haven't seemed to be working out.

In December 2024, I was invited to speak on an alumni panel at EducationUSA. The event was held in Lagos, Nigeria, in January 2025. On that panel, I shared more about my journey, the lessons I have learned, the obstacles I faced, and the ways I have grown since coming to the U.S. I hoped to guide students applying to schools in the U.S., and as I sat behind the table, facing the audience of seventy to eighty people, I was reminded of how five years ago, I was sitting right in that hall, listening to others share their journeys.

It was an emotional reminder of how far I had come and how much my life had changed since coming to the U.S. I truly had so much to be grateful for.

About two weeks later, I made a post on my WhatsApp status saying that fifty years from that time, I hoped to still vividly remember the electric feeling I got when I received my acceptance letter to Bowdoin. It was a life-changing email, and I will forever be grateful for the opportunity to learn, grow, and become in a place like this.

Forgetting is the easiest thing in the world.

It's easy to forget how far we've come when things are not going as planned, and I have experienced this time and time again. When we are in waiting seasons, we often don't remember all we have received and how we might have once hoped for the things we currently have. Forgetting is part of our nature as humans, which is why intentionally practicing gratitude is so important.

Throughout my time at Bowdoin, I had to remind myself that I was living in answered prayers. During my gap years before admission, I had prayed for months on end for my admission and about my journey to the U.S. I would watch those *Day in My Life* videos of students at different colleges, hoping that one day, I, too, would experience what it was like to go to college in the U.S. The very things I was worried about, now that I was in college, now that I had them, were an indication that I was no longer where I used to be.

Take a moment to think of the fact that you also might be living in answered prayers.

Tips for staying grateful:

Remember that you've been given all you have:

It's the perfect tonic for uprooting pride, arrogance, and a false sense of self-sufficiency. It's the perfect tonic for instilling gratitude. Yes, you worked hard. But yes, all that you have is a gift. Every opportunity. Every chance. Every good relationship. Every person who willingly helped you. All you have is a gift.

Keep a gratitude journal:

You'll need it on the hard days and during the hard seasons. When everything around seems to be withering and you're nearly enveloped with uncertainty, it helps to look back and remember that God has seen you through equally or even drier seasons. Like I said, when we're faced with tough times, we forget the good times. Keeping a journal ensures you have reminders when your mind runs blank and can't recall the goodness of God. One important thing: Be specific when writing your gratitude list

Volunteer or give back:

Helping others can help increase your sense of gratitude. I heard someone say that we ought to be flowing streams and not stagnant waters, meaning that as God's goodness flows into our lives, we ought to let that goodness flow from us to others. What's more? The memory of how we've been a blessing to others will, amongst other things, come back to comfort us. Psalms 41:1 affirms this: "Oh, the joys of those who are kind to the poor! The Lord rescues them when they are in trouble."

Remember the small things too:

Like the man who gave you his seat on the train the day your legs could hardly carry you, and the miraculous delay that ensured you submitted your assignment on time. Those small things, when you take a good look at them, will remind you that you've never been abandoned. They'll inspire gratitude.

Lastly, occasionally, reflect on how far you have come.

Having an attitude of gratitude has helped me throughout my time at Bowdoin, and I encourage you to practice it. I know it's easier said than done, especially when we're in tough seasons of our lives, but I hope that this chapter encourages you to try.

Please make your notes here:

CHAPTER 20

The process of applying to U.S. colleges

"The journey of a thousand miles begins with one step."

—Lao Tzu

I have come an incredibly long way, but sometimes in the busyness of all my engagements and the pursuit of my ambitions, I forget to acknowledge how far fifteen-year-old Ruth, who was fresh out of high school, has come.

After writing all the chapters of this book, I realized I still had one important piece to add: the process of applying to schools in the U.S. In this chapter, I will share what the process of applying to U.S. colleges was like, the individual components, and some of the important documents I used.

While I hope this chapter can offer insights for those who don't know where to start or are stuck in one part of the process, it is difficult for me to capture all the nuances of the application process in one chapter. My experiences might be different from what you will encounter as you apply. Various factors can influence what the process will be like for you. Factors like your finances, your high school, whether you know anyone who has gone to the U.S. to study, and more.

EducationUSA's vital role in my journey.

I cannot speak about my journey to the U.S. without mentioning EducationUSA, Lagos. This organization helped me understand the complex process of applying to schools in the U.S., provided support as I studied for the Scholastic Aptitude Test (SAT), helped me prepare for the more than twelve interviews I did, and shared important resources for other parts of the process.

EducationUSA is a global network of international student advising centers that are supported by the U.S. Department of State. EducationUSA has over four hundred and thirty advising centers in more than one hundred and seventy-five countries. These advising centers provide accurate and comprehensive information about U.S. colleges and universities, including what their admission requirements are, the academic programs they offer, and financial aid.

In the chapter on maximizing opportunities, I spoke about how in 2019, I applied to EducationUSA Lagos' annual Opportunity Funds Program (OFP), a scholarship that provides guidance and financial support to high-achieving low-income students applying to study in the United States. This program was incredibly helpful, not just for the guidance it gave me, but for the financial burden it helped my family avoid while I was applying to schools. The OFP program covered the cost of my SAT and Passport when I began applying and then paid for my Visa and flight ticket to the U.S. when I got admitted into Bowdoin.

EducationUSA is the organization I always recommend first to students in Nigeria when they reach out to ask about where they can get resources and guidance on how to apply to U.S. colleges and universities. There is a membership fee to join EducationUSA Lagos and access the plethora of resources, but because I was an OFP scholar, this fee was covered for me.

If you would like to join EducationUSA but the fee is a barrier, they host several free events that you can partake in. They include online workshops and events with U.S. colleges and universities, as well as their online or in-person college fairs. Their weekly *General Orientation* is also a free event you can attend if you need help with getting the general overview of the process of applying to schools in the U.S.

There are many ways people approach applying to schools in the U.S., but I will give a brief description of what I learned through EducationUSA, which was the process I followed.

1. Conducting my research:

There are thousands of colleges and universities in the U.S. These schools come in various sizes (large, medium, or small), are located in different parts of the country, offer various degrees, and have different testing and essay requirements. As a result, the first thing I had to do was research what kinds of schools I wanted to go to.

I remember sitting on my sister's couch when I filled out the EducationUSA form about what kind of school I wanted to go to, whether a school in an urban or rural area, whether I wanted large or small class sizes, how much financial aid I would need, and the rest. I spent months doing my research, and this happened while I prepared for the SAT and when I had started crafting my essays for some schools.

I searched for schools that would foster my academic growth, had close communities, offered lots of resources to their students, and, very importantly, could give me significant financial aid. All these were factors I kept in mind as I started my application process.

Doing your research is a foundational part of your application journey because it will help you ensure you are applying to schools you truly want to attend and see yourself as a good fit for; schools that can meet your needs. Investing as much time and energy into this process will save you time and money in the long run.

2. Financing my study:

When I began applying to schools in the U.S. in 2019, the exchange rate was about one Dollar to 365 Naira (which, as of 2025, has quadrupled). I vividly remember plugging in these numbers into the College Scholarship Service Profile (CSS) and International Student Financial Aid Application (ISFAA), both applications with which I applied for financial aid from the schools. With this conversation rate, I knew I would be unable to afford attending a school in the U.S. without financial aid. Financial aid includes scholarships, grants, work-study, and loans that make college more affordable.

As I began applying to schools, I had to ensure the schools I was applying to could give me the amount of financial support I needed. I soon found out that schools that could give significant financial aid to international students, especially grants and scholarships (which are financial aid options you don't have to pay back), were very competitive. These schools were already competitive for U.S. students, let alone foreign students like me who can't access U.S. federal student aid. Knowing how competitive these schools were early was important for how I approached the application process and helped me remember to put my best foot forward.

To apply for financial aid, I needed my parents' bank statements and records of all their financial documents, which were items I was unfamiliar with. Once I knew all the documents I needed, I explained to my parents all I needed and gave them enough time to gather the documents while I was working on my application. This is something you would need to do early on in the process.

3. Completing my applications:

Once I did my research for schools, their programs, their admission requirements, and the financial aid package they offered, I began applying. This application spanned a year and a half, since I applied to schools twice. In those two application cycles, I prepared my applications to various schools through an online application called Common App. Common App is an online application that allows students to apply to colleges and universities worldwide. With the Common App, you can complete only one core application and then customize it for every school with additional information each school requests. This platform was vital for my application process and was what I used to apply to a majority of schools.

To apply, I uploaded my SAT results, high school transcripts, and West African Examination Council (WAEC) exam results, wrote a personal statement and numerous school-specific essays, and participated in multiple interviews. There were sections in the Common App that asked about my most meaningful extracurricular activities and commitments while in high school, my awards or honors, and other information colleges needed to understand who I was as an applicant.

This process was long and exhausting because there were many things I had to learn on the go. I had never had to think about my participation in extracurricular activities like I had to while applying, and telling my story through multiple essays was something I hadn't done before. This process required that I ask questions even when I was afraid to, try things that were very new to me, and believe that things would work out for me.

There were nights when I would sit awake in my room at two a.m. so I could join an information session with a school; afternoons where I would spend time working on my essays at EducationUSA; or evenings when I sat at the dining table to have my interview. I remember a particular evening when my phone went off a few minutes before the end of an interview because I had not been able to charge my phone enough due to the unstable electricity in the community where I lived. But despite the limited resources I had, I still submitted all my applications when I needed to.

4. Applying for my student visa:

When my admission eventually came in and I had accepted my

spot as a member of Bowdoin's class of 2025, I had to familiarize myself with the U.S. student visa requirements. I started doing this while I waited for my admission decision, because I knew the visa process usually took months. Thankfully, EducationUSA held informative sessions to guide us through the logistics and important information we needed for preparing our visa applications and for our visa interviews.

5. Preparing for my departure:

The final step to beginning my study in the U.S. was preparing to travel to the U.S. as soon as my student visa was approved.

EducationUSA Lagos organized a pre-departure orientation for all the students who were traveling to start their graduate or undergraduate studies. Here, we spoke about culture shock, adjusting to college life, building a community, getting involved on campus, dealing with homesickness, and more. Having a pre-departure orientation was a vital piece, as it helped prepare my mind for the transition.

Another important thing I did was connect with four Nigerian students who were at Bowdoin at the time. Ruby, Adedunmola, Onyedika, and Chiamaka were eager to answer my questions about college life, being a Nigerian student at Bowdoin, getting involved on campus, and more. Speaking with them set me up to make the best use of all Bowdoin had to offer, and I will forever be grateful to the four of them for creating a sense of community for me before I even left the shores of Nigeria.

The struggles of applying.

The application process was far from easy for me. I had no precedent in my family for studying in the U.S., nor did I have anyone close by to guide me, so this was a new experience for me and my family, as they supported me in the ways they could. Looking back, I'm so incredibly proud of how teenage Ruth persevered despite the roadblocks she faced, some of which I share below.

I lived with my parents in Ikorodu, Lagos, during my two gap years, and because of how far our home was from EducationUSA Lagos' center in Victoria Island, Lagos, there were many days I would wake up at five am to be able to catch the bus from home to the center and beat Lagos' traffic. This started when I was only fifteen years old, and I would leave the house when it was still pitch dark so that I could get to the center in time for events that were being held. These events included panels with admitted students, essay workshops, interview prep, and more. Since EducationUSA was my biggest source of advising, I did all it took to make sure I could maximize all the resources they provided, even if it meant waking up at five am and standing on the bus for a majority of my journey from Ikorodu to Victoria Island.

I did not know anything about the SAT before joining EducationUSA other than it was an exam people wrote when they wanted to apply to schools in the U.S. It was not until I was accepted into the OFP program that I learned of the technicalities involved in the exam, the contents it covered, how long it was, where to access practice exams, and other important details. As a result, by the time I took the SAT, I had done only about a month of preparation. For context, some people start preparing for the SAT in their second year of high school, and many people start preparing at least a year before they take the exam, but I prepared for only about a month with limited resources.

The day before I took my SAT, I had to pick up my Passport document with a few of my friends who were a part of my OPT cohort. We didn't have our passports and couldn't write the exam without them, so EducationUSA paid for our passports, and they were processed with barely enough time for us to pick them up before our exam.

As we all returned to our various homes that night, I sat at the back of a bus, exhausted from the day's journey and thinking of how I would have to wake up early the next day to go to the center where I would write my exam. It was nerve-wracking because I felt tired and underprepared. Could I have a little more time to rest, to study? I couldn't. The day was already around the corner.

I did write my SAT the next day and was glad I had gotten it over with, but I was not satisfied with how it went. When the results came out, I couldn't bring myself to check immediately. My heart was pounding as I looked at the email announcing that my results were ready. Eventually, I opened it, and my heart sank to my stomach. It wasn't up to what I was expecting. However, it was good enough for me to apply.

About one year later, I decided to take the SAT again, but I decided too close to the date of the exam, so my preparation was just as short (or maybe even shorter) than the first time, and I got a score lower than the first score. So, I decided to use my first SAT score to apply to schools.

Throughout the application process, I did not have a laptop. So, I would write my college essays on the Microsoft Word app on my phone. Yes, on my phone. Imagine me zooming into my phone and typing in my essays with the tiny keyboard because it was all I had, and I had to make the most of it. Whenever I needed to use a computer to write an essay or access any site that was best viewed with a desktop view, like my financial portal, I would either go to a cyber cafe or make a trip to EducationUSA Lagos.

There are many internal and external struggles I faced throughout that season that I haven't mentioned, but despite all of them, I didn't stop dreaming, working hard, and giving my best. Just like my elder brother said, one yes could change my life. It sure did!

Like I mentioned earlier, the process of applying to schools in the U.S. was long and demanding and had many parts. While I could not capture everything in this chapter, I hope all the insights I shared offer you guidance. And if you have been struggling with believing you can study in the U.S. because you don't know anyone who has ever done it, I hope that reading this book has made you feel like you now do.

If you have more questions about how I came to study in the U.S. and how you can do it too, please send me an email here: rutholujobi01@gmail.com. I'll be glad to help or link you up with someone who can help you better.

Cheers, dear dreamer. I hope you never lose your passion.

Please make your notes here:

A NOTE FROM THE AUTHOR

I wrote most of this book in my final semester of college—one of the most fulfilling but intense seasons of my life. Between classes, graduation prep, leadership commitments, countless job applications, multiple projects, and a flood of emotions that come with closing one chapter and anticipating the next, I often felt like I was holding many things at once. And many times, I was.

I cried more that semester than in my other college semesters. It was a time of deep gratitude but also a time of immense stretching. There were nights at two a.m. when I would alternate between searching for jobs, completing class assignments, and writing a chapter of this book. For months, I sat with uncertainty, not knowing where I'd be after graduation or what doors would open. As an international student, those questions weren't just emotional; they were logistical, legal, and urgent. But amid everything, I kept writing.

What I didn't fully realize until near the end was that this book had become a companion to me throughout that semester. In many ways, it was my way of holding on to the lessons, the laughter, the tears, and the growth I experienced over the last four years. It reminded me of how far I've come and how much beauty can emerge when we choose to keep showing up, even when things feel uncertain.

I wanted to wait until every part of this book felt flawless and "complete" before releasing it. But I realized that part of what makes *Dear Sojourner* real and special is that it doesn't come from a place of perfection—it comes from my journey of *becoming,* a journey I'm still on.

Even in its finished state, this book captures only a fraction of my experiences and lessons in college—I couldn't possibly fit them all into these pages.

This book is a product of lots of prayers, heartfelt conversations, unwavering support, hard work, late nights, and countless quiet moments of courage. Despite the odds, we did it. This book is in your hands, and I couldn't be more grateful!

I hope that this book is the gift I meant it to be, and that my journey offers you valuable lessons that will stay with you.

I'm cheering you on.

Ruth Olujobi.
May 2025.

ACKNOWLEDGEMENTS

My deepest gratitude goes to God, the One who knew me even before I was born. I would not be here without His grace, guidance, and wisdom.

I'm incredibly thankful for my parents, Mr. Daniel and Mrs. Florence Olujobi, for their unwavering support over the years. Throughout my time at Bowdoin, they did their best to support me however they could. I remember the night in February of my senior year when I called them and unexpectedly burst into tears a few minutes into our call. This was the first time, during my entire stay at Bowdoin, that I would be crying on a call with them. I was so overwhelmed by having to juggle school demands, job search, several leadership commitments, work, planning for post-grad life, and much more. They lovingly reminded me that they were praying for me and that things would turn out better than I could see in that moment.

My siblings, Grace, Emmanuel, Joseph, Paul, and Stephen, have also been a great source of support for me, cheering me on as I navigated college, listening to me share my aspirations, offering guidance, and reminding me of how far I've come.

I don't think my sister knows how much her decision to connect me with the Obis impacted my time in college.

When I first had the vision, in my sophomore year, to write this book, I immediately shared it with Emmanuel and Stephen. They helped nurture this dream even when I didn't think I could continue. The summer after my sophomore year, I had a long call with Joseph where we spoke extensively about steps I could take to start writing this book. When I eventually began writing, Stephen was one of my first editors, and he gave me priceless feedback that led me to where we are now.

They say it takes a village to raise a child. My village contains many families that have nurtured me in more ways than I can outline in this book. I hold deep gratitude for Mr. Tony and Mrs. Bertha Nwozor for raising me as their daughter and fostering my dreams to explore the world.

From the moment I arrived in the U.S., Mr. Charles and Mrs. Funmi Obi welcomed me into their home with so much love. Their home truly was a home-away-from-home.

Susan and Ben, my Bowdoin host parents, opened their home to me and were also an important source of support throughout my time at Bowdoin.

EducationUSA Lagos created a space for me to work towards my dream of studying in the U.S. and provided the resources I needed to make that dream a reality. I'm grateful to Mrs. Chinenye Uwadileke and Mrs. Adeola Adejumobi, who served as my advisors during the application process. I'm grateful to all my peers with whom I went on this journey.

My friends mean the world to me, and I feel so blessed to be surrounded by such amazing people. A special thank you to Daniel Afolabi and Bukola Adewuyi, two of my wonderful friends who also served as my first editors. They saw this book in its rawest form, when many of my thoughts were not fully fleshed out and I didn't know all I wanted to say. They were also a huge support for navigating the complexities of being a first-time author and balancing writing a book with other responsibilities.

Promise Akpan, who has been Blooming Daily's brand designer since our launch in 2022, was eager to work on the book's designs. Esther Akinyemi, my very good friend since secondary school, excitedly agreed to build a website to house the book. Erioluwa Adeyinka was always available to answer my questions on the best ways for me to complete writing this book and plan for its launch while balancing the many other things on my plate. Their support was truly invaluable.

I'm honored to have had Ikanna Okim write the foreword to this book. The day I reached out to her, she did not hesitate to accept my request. When I shared my dream to write this book with her almost two years prior, she gave me valuable advice that would prove helpful when I finally started writing. Ikanna is one of the many mentor figures who guided me throughout my time at Bowdoin, and I will always be grateful to have learned from the experiences of such phenomenal people.

I'm also very grateful to my editor, Brown Patience, for her incredible work with the book. She understood my vision for the book the very first day we spoke about it, and despite the tight timeline we had, she made things work.

As I reflect on how much I learned at Bowdoin, I'm so thankful to have studied under many incredible professors. Professor Manuel Diaz-Rios, my Major Advisor, made it possible for me to conduct research at Bowdoin and was a constant support throughout my four years. Professor Jens Klenner was my Pre-major Advisor and a big influence on why I decided to learn German, and I will always be grateful to him for helping me step into that whole new world. Professor Birgit Tautz and Professor Jill Smith, two other German professors, made me love the German department even more, and they always had their doors open to me. Professor Zahir Janmohamed was the first professor I took a fiction-writing class with. I loved it so much that I was always thinking of creative writing. And because it was the semester before I fully started writing this book, his class helped me get into a good momentum for the months of intense writing that followed.

Countless people have influenced my life in many ways and made it possible for me to be where I am today. From my family, incredible friends at home and abroad, my church communities, my awesome professors, the staff at all the offices I worked at or interacted with while at Bowdoin, and my supporters and acquaintances around the world. The list is inexhaustible. I'm deeply grateful to every one of you!

Made in United States
North Haven, CT
05 September 2025

72560295R10122